CHECK YOUR ENGLISH VOCABULARY FOR

TOEIC®

by

Rawdon Wyatt

BLOOMSBURY

First published in Great Britain 2006, reprinted 2009, by A & C Black Publishers Ltd

This second edition published 2012 by

Bloomsbury Publishing Plc
50 Bedford Square
London
WC1B 3DP
www.bloomsbury.com

A CIP record for this book is available from the British Library.

ISBN: 978-1-4081-5391-8

This book is produced using paper that is made from wood grown in managed,
sustainable forests. It is natural, renewable and recyclable.
The logging and manufacturing processes conform to the environmental
regulations of the country of origin.

Typeset by Saxon Graphics Ltd, Derby
Printed and bound in Great Britain by MPG Books Limited

Introduction

This book has been written for anyone who is planning to take the TOEIC®, exam and who wants to practice and develop their vocabulary. A greater command of vocabulary is one of the key factors that will help you raise your TOEIC® score.

You should not go through the exercises in this book mechanically. It is better to choose areas that you are unfamiliar with, or areas that you feel are of specific interest or importance to yourself.

Each exercise is accompanied by a full answer key at the back of the book. This key also gives you other information about particular vocabulary items (for example, words with similar meanings, alternative words and expressions, etc) that are not covered in the exercises themselves.

When you are doing the tasks in this book, look at the instructions carefully to make sure you understand what to do, then read through the text / questions first before attempting the exercises. This is a useful "skimming" technique that you should also use when you are doing the TOEIC® itself.

We recommend that you have a good dictionary with you, and refer to it when necessary. However, always try to do the exercises *without* a dictionary first, and then use the dictionary to check anything that you are not sure of. A particularly useful reference is the *Macmillan English Dictionary for Advanced Learners*. You will find a free on line version of this at www. macmillandictionary.com. When you open the web page, make sure you choose 'American', which you will find by clicking on 'Options' at the top of the page.

It is very important to keep a record of new words and expressions that you learn, and review these on a regular basis so that they become a part of your "active" vocabulary. Unless you are taking the TOEIC® Test of Spoken English, the TOEIC® is an exam which tests your language *recognition* skills rather than your language *production* skills. However, if you familiarize yourself with the vocabulary in the book by reviewing it and then trying to use it in your written and spoken English on a regular basis, you will be in a better position to recognize it if and when it comes up in the exam.

No vocabulary book can possibly contain all of the words and expressions that you are likely to meet in the TOEIC® exam, so it is important you acquire new vocabulary from other sources. Try to read as much as possible from a different variety of authentic reading materials (books, newspapers, journals, magazines, on line articles, etc), and familiarize yourself with spoken English by listening to English-language radio stations and watching English-language films and television programs whenever possible.

Try to get plenty of exam practice before you do the exam itself, so that you become familiar with the format. There are several books, courses and other publications that will help you. Barron's *TOEIC®* by Dr. Lin Lougheed (ISBN 978-0-7641-4557-5), which contains lots of helpful advice as well as complete model tests, is particularly useful. You might also like to consider Barron's *TOEIC® Practice Exams* by the same author (ISBN 978-0-7641-9784-0).

We hope you enjoy doing the exercises in this book and that they help you to practice and develop the vocabulary that you need. Good luck in the TOEIC®!

Contents

Exercise 1

Complete the second sentence in each sentence pair below with a word or phrase from the box so that its meaning is similar to the first sentence. There are some words / phrases in the box that do not fit in any of the sentences. Note that you do <u>not</u> need to change any word forms.

---

build up   constant rise   cuts   dramatic increase   expansion   general improvement
phased in   phased out   sharp decline / fall   steady decrease   strengthening
tightening up   weakening   widening

---

1. Last year, 33% of the population worked in secondary industries and 48% worked in the tertiary sector. This year, the figures are 27% and 53% respectively.
    There has been a .... of the gap between those working in different sectors of the economy.

2. Last year, the overseas market accounted for 60% of our sales. This year, it only accounts for about 15%.
    There has been a .... in overseas sales figures in the last year.

3. People can afford to buy more and live more comfortably than they could twenty years ago.
    There has been a .... in the standard of living.

4. Because our company is bigger now than it was two years ago, we need to recruit more employees.
    Because of company .... over the last two years, we need more workers.

5. American travelers abroad have discovered that they can buy more foreign currency with their dollar.
    There has been a .... of the dollar.

6. It is now much harder to import goods into the country than it was a few years ago.
    There has been a .... of border controls for imports.

7. In 2008 inflation was running at about 4%, in 2009 it was 4.5%, in 2010 it was 5% and in 2011 it was 5.5%.
    Between 2008 and 2011, there was a .... in the rate of inflation.

8. Last year, the company employed 200 people. This year it now has over 1,000 employees.
    There has been a .... in the number of employees working for the company.

9. Unemployment figures have dropped by about 2% every year for the last four years.
    There has been a .... in unemployment figures over the last four years.

10. Over the next few years, some management positions in the company will be gradually removed.
    Some management positions will be .... over the next few years.

11. Because of forecasts for high demand in the future, we need to increase our stocks.
    We need to .... our stocks to cope with future demand.

12. The government will spend less on the welfare system next year.
    There are going to be .... in welfare spending next year.

Exercise 2

Now do the same with these.

> amended   broaden   considerable growth   deterioration   downsizing
> downward trend   fluctuated   marked progress   reduce   restructure   slipped
> streamline   upgrade   upward trend

1. Public services are less reliable now than they were five years ago.
   There has been a .... in public services reliability over the last five years.

2. Nowadays, more and more people are traveling abroad for business and pleasure.
   There has been .... in the overseas travel market.

3. Compared with five years ago, more people are shopping in out-of-town malls than in local stores.
   There has been an .... in the number of people shopping in out-of-town malls.

4. Unless your work visibly improves, we will have to recommend a transfer to another department.
   We need to see some .... in your work, or we will recommend a departmental transfer.

5. Young Americans want to travel, meet new people and see more of the world than their parents and grandparents did.
   Young Americans want to .... their horizons.

6. Over the next two months, we plan to make our office computers faster and more efficient.
   Over the next two months, we plan to .... our office computers.

7. We are trying to make the accounting system simpler and more efficient.
   We are trying to .... the accounting system.

8. Making the company smaller by making a lot of staff members redundant has made it much more profitable than it was before.
   ... the company has made it much more profitable than it was before.

9. Standards of service have gone down recently, and as a result we have lost a lot of customers.
   Standards of service have .... recently, and as a result we have lost a lot of customers.

10. This year, property prices have gone up, then gone down, then risen again, and then fallen a second time.
    Property prices have .... this year.

11. We have made small changes to the rules for applying for instant credit.
    We have .... the rules for applying for instant credit.

12. The company is planning to change its marketing division to make it more effective.
    The company is planning to .... its marketing division.

Also see *Changes 2* on page 3.

The box below contains 28 words used to describe change in different situations. These are all verbs, and they can be found by reading from left to right and from right to left, starting in the top-left corner and following the direction of the arrows. Separate these words, then use some of them to complete sentences 1 – 12 below. In some cases you will need to change the form of the verb (for example, by putting it into its past simple or past participle form).

⇨	a	d	a	p	t	r	e	p	l	a	c	e	e	x	p	a	n	d	i	n
	t	e	c	u	d	e	r	e	t	o	m	o	r	p	e	s	a	e	r	c
	r	a	n	s	f	o	r	m	s	w	i	t	c	h	r	e	n	o	v	a
	e	t	l	a	e	t	o	m	e	d	e	g	n	a	h	c	x	e	e	t
	r	d	i	s	a	p	p	e	a	r	v	a	r	y	r	a	i	s	e	l
	i	e	h	e	g	r	a	l	n	e	d	n	e	t	x	e	r	e	w	o
	g	h	t	e	n	l	e	n	g	t	h	e	n	w	i	d	e	n	d	e
	e	r	h	c	t	e	r	t	s	n	e	t	r	o	h	s	n	e	p	e
	v	i	s	e	f	a	l	l	o	u	t	s	o	u	r	c	e	d	i	s
															e	v	l	o	s

1.   The company cannot refund customers' money, and goods can only be .... on production of a receipt or other proof of purchase.

2.   We have made radical changes to workplace regulations, and employees are expected to .... to these over the next few weeks.

3.   Our customer call center used to be in Wichita, but last year we .... it to India, where costs are much lower.

4.   The new director has completely .... the company, from a small local enterprise to a major international concern.

5.   The hotel is currently being ...., but will remain open while building work is carried out.

6.   Production has been .... from our Boston site to a new industrial center outside of Portland.

7.   Our new memory sticks .... in price, from $8 for a 2Gb stick up to $22 for a 16Gb one.

8.   The Internet clothing company Pants-2-U.com has .... its range to include jewelry and watches.

9.   The decision to .... the company wasn't an easy one to make, but everyone agreed that there was no other option but to cease trading.

10.   Air fares will be .... on 21 July: domestic flights will go down by 10%, but international flights will go up by 22%.

11.   A college course can help you find work or get ....

12.   The guarantee is for 12 months from date of purchase, but for $50, customers can .... it to 36 months.

Also see *Changes 1* on pages 1 and 2.

Comparing and contrasting

Complete these sentences with the most appropriate word or phrase in **bold** which you will see at the end of each sentence. In one case, all three options are possible.

1. The .... in working conditions between our Denver department and our department in Chicago is very noticeable, and employees are now demanding equality in this area. **contrast / compare / comparison**

2. The two companies .... considerably from each other: one sells to the wholesale market, and one sells directly to retailers. **differentiate / differ / different**

3. It is often difficult to .... between employees who are off work because they are genuinely ill, and those who are just enjoying a day at home. **differentiate / differ / contrast**

4. Our new software program shares some common .... with those that are already on the market. **characters / characterizes / characteristics**

5. There's a clear .... between starting your own company, and taking over one that already exists. **distinguish / distinctive / distinction**

6. .... with 15 years ago, home computers are cheaper, faster and have a much bigger memory. **Compared / Compare / Comparing**

7. The two products are different in every way: there's absolutely no .... between them. **compare / comparison / contrast**

8. Our latest cellphones .... those of our main competitor, except that they have more features and are more reliable. **similar to / alike / resemble**

9. There are several .... between our new photocopier and our old one: these include an advanced color facility and a multitask option. **similarities / similarly / similar to**

10. Serious computer hackers can access your personal files and destroy or alter them. ...., they can gain access to your Internet banking facility and steal your money. **Exactly / In the same way / Just as**

11. The quality of our products is unbeatable. ...., the price. **Likewise / Alike / Likeness**

12. The TOEFL exam covers a variety of general English tasks. ...., the TOEIC focuses more on business and professional issues. **In contrast to / Although / By way of contrast**

13. The company has not performed very well during the last quarter. ....….., it has still managed to turn a profit and retain most of its clients. **Nevertheless / Even so / However**

14. There currently seems to be a large .... between the number of people employed in service industries, and those employed in the primary sector. **discrepancy / discrimination / differential**

15. Our new contract states that both parties must give six months' notice of termination, ... our old contract had an immediate "get-out" clause. **unlike / whereas / whereby**

Computers and information technology

Exercise 1

Read the passage below, in which someone is talking about their computer. Unfortunately, they have used some language which is not very technical. Replace the words and phrases in **bold** with something more appropriate from the box.

CD drive   components   CPU (Central Processing Unit)   desktop PC DTP (desktop publishing)   hard disk   hard drive   keyboard   laptop   load memory   memory stick   monitor   mouse   printer   scanner   software spreadsheet   USB port   word processing

This is my new (1) **computer that sits on top of a table or desk** .... (I've also got a (2) **small computer which can be carried and held on your knees** ....). As you can see, there are six main (3) **parts** .... to it. The first is the (4) **part of the computer that runs it and controls what it does** ...., and this is the most important bit. It carries the (5) **part that stores and controls the flow of information** ...., including the (6) **round thing that is used for storing information** .... Mine has a particularly high (7) **capacity for storing information** ...., which means that it's much faster than most. It came with its own (8) **computer programs** .... package (including (9) **writing, checking and changing texts** ...., (10) **calculating in columns of figures** ...., and (11) **producing texts and pictures for magazines** .... packages). You can also (12) **put in** .... other programs using the (13) **sliding tray for carrying round, plastic, information-holding things** ...., or the (14) **hole for connecting computer parts to one another** .... (into which you can put a (15) **small plastic and metal stick which can hold a lot of information** ....). The other five parts of the computer are the (16) **screen that lets you see what your computer is doing** ...., the (17) **flat thing with the letters and numbers on it that let you control the computer** ...., the (18) **machine that lets you make copies of the documents that you create on your computer** ...., the (19) **device for making color copies of photographs and other documents which you can put onto your computer** .... and, last but not least, the (20) **device that you hold in your hand and move across your desk to control the cursor** ....

Exercise 2

Now do the same with the next part of the passage.

access   antivirus software   attachment   bookmark   browser   chat rooms crashing   delete   download   email   homepage   Internet   keywords links   log on   log out   on line   pop-up   provider   search engine spam   update   virus   Web site

Now, in my opinion, the best thing about modern information technology is the (1) **network that links millions of computers from around the world** .... Once you've got yourself a (2) **company** .... that allows you (3) **entry** ...., and a (4) **program that finds information** ...., you can start using this. It's especially useful if you want to get information about something, go shopping or (5) **transfer** .... information, games, music, etc, onto your own computer. You can even "talk" to other computer users in (6) **special places where you can leave messages and get instant replies** .... Most companies have their own (7) **special computer pages** .... which you can look at. Let me (8) **turn the computer on, enter my code and access the computer system** ...., and I'll show you ours. OK, here we go. Oh no, another (9) **advertisement that suddenly appears on the computer screen** .... How annoying. Let me just remove it. That's better.

Now, I can never remember the exact address of our company, so first of all I'll type it into the (10) **program that helps you find the information you want** .... OK, "Bloomsbury Publishing'. The computer identifies the (11) **most important or main words** .... and then gives me (12) **connections** .... to a list of possible sites. This one looks right: "www.bloomsbury.com". I'll click on that. Bingo! Here's our (13) **front page** .... You can use this to find the different books that we publish, and you can even buy them (14) **through the computer** .... Hmm, this book looks good: "Check your English Vocabulary for TOEIC'. Now, before I (15) **exit this site** ...., I'll just (16) **add it to my list of favorites** .... so that I can find it more quickly next time.

Perhaps the most important thing, however, is (17) **a special electronic letter-sending facility** ...., which allows you to communicate with people around the world in an instant. Let me quickly check mine. Oh dear, nothing very interesting. Mainly a load of (18) **unwanted advertising** .... I'll just (19) **remove** .... it: I don't particularly want to rent a vacation home in Mexico, have my future read by one of America's top astrologers or join a casino. There's something here from my sister with a / an (20) **document or file that has been sent with it** .... You have to be careful with these: sometimes they contain a (21) **hidden routine placed in the program that destroys or corrupts files** .... If you open it, it can do all sorts of horrible things to your computer. I had one last week that kept (22) **shutting down** .... my computer. I do have some (23) **stuff on my computer that protects it from such things** ...., but it's a bit out of date: I really ought to (24) **renew** .... it.

The exercises above contain just a few of the words and expressions related to computers and information technology. Many more enter our vocabulary each year. How many others do you know?

Condition and requirement

Rearrange the letters in **bold** to make words and phrases related to condition and requirement. The first one has been done as an example.

1. **sA nlgo sa** _As long as_ customers continue to demand the BD17 model mobile, Telelink will continue to produce it. If demand falls, the line will be discontinued.

2. **seUsln** .... we receive your payment within ten days, we will have to start charging you interest.

3. We will continue to offer you interest-free credit **no incotnido atth** .... you maintain regular repayments to your account. The minimum monthly repayment is $250.

4. Everyone will get a raise this month **vogrnipid ttha** .... we meet our sales targets.

5. The main **retncopiinod** .... for increased consumer spending is a stable economy with low inflation and low interest rates. Without these, people will save rather than spend.

6. (Notice on a fire alarm): **nl eacs fo** .... fire, break glass.

7. **nl het nvete fo** .... a delay to their flight, all passengers will receive a voucher for a light meal at the airport.

8. We agreed to sign the contract, the only **aputonstili** .... being that it would run for at least five years.

9. The management has **nidncoalitoun** .... trust in its employees: it knows they will do their best at all times, even if things get difficult.

10. **sumsAgin hatt** .... your flight is on time, we will meet you at LaGuardia airport at ten o'clock.

11. We will proceed with the delivery of spare parts **no teh autonmsspi hatt** .... your order has remained unchanged.

12. Being able to drive is one of the **quereesisitpr** .... of the job: if you cannot drive, you will not be considered for the post.

13. Before you accept a job, it is important that you agree with the **remst** .... and **ioctnsodin** .... set out in the contract.

14. It is a **nmreiretque** .... of the company that employees have a medical at least once a year.

15. If you have a query, telephone us at the number above. **niiFagl ttha** .... send us an email.

16. We need to involve at least 20 people on this project, **ehewotris** .... it can't go ahead.

Confusing words

The sentences below are all missing one word. Four possible answers follow each sentence. Choose the best answer in each case. Note that each set of answers includes some words that are often confused with one another, either because: (a) they are related to the same topic, but have a different meaning; (b) they look similar but have a different meaning; (c) they are the wrong form of the word needed; (d) they are English words which have a similar-looking word in another language but which have a different meaning (we call these words *false friends*).

1. Try to make your report as .... as possible: only give us the facts, and not your opinions.
    (a) **subjective**   (b) **objectionable**   (c) **subjected**   (d) **objective**

2. Environmental inspectors regularly .... our kitchens and other food preparation areas to make sure they conform to regulations.
    (a) **inspect**   (b) **control**   (c) **study**   (d) **analyze**

3. .... workers are often rewarded with higher salaries and other benefits.
    (a) **Conscious**   (b) **Conscientious**   (c) **Conscience**   (d) **Consciousness**

4. Airlines are already increasing their prices on the .... that fuel prices are going to rise.
    (a) **consumption**   (b) **destruction**   (c) **assumption**   (d) **presumption**

5. The fire caused a lot of .... to the building and factory machinery.
    (a) **damage**   (b) **harm**   (c) **injury**   (d) **wound**

6. Government subsidies helped to .... many companies being forced to close down.
    (a) **prevent**   (b) **preventive**   (c) **avoidance**   (d) **avoid**

7. The manager made it clear that he intended to .... down some new rules to enforce workplace discipline.
    (a) **lying**   (b) **lie**   (c) **laying**   (d) **lay**

8. Cuts in advertising will have a serious .... on sales.
    (a) **effective**   (b) **effect**   (c) **affect**   (d) **affection**

9. If you want to take photographs, you will need to apply for a ....
    (a) **permit**   (b) **permission**   (c) **permissible**   (d) **permitting**

10. At the meeting, the manager talked .... about the need for better attendance and punctuality.
    (a) **briefly**   (b) **briefing**   (c) **shortly**   (d) **shorts**

11. The office will be closed .... it is being decorated.
    (a) **during**   (b) **while**   (c) **for**   (d) **throughout**

12. Can you .... me on the best course of action to take?
    (a) **advisory**   (b) **advisable**   (c) **advice**   (d) **advise**

13. Economic .... slowly stagnated as the recession became worse.
    (a) **active**   (b) **action**   (c) **activity**   (d) **activist**

14. .... their regular daytime job, many people do extra work in the evening.
    (a) **By**   (b) **Beside**   (c) **Between**   (d) **Besides**

15. The computer system crashed on Monday, then again on Wednesday and finally today. If it keeps giving us .... problems like this, we'll have to replace it.
    (a) **continuing**   (b) **continuous**   (c) **continuation**   (d) **continual**

Exercise 2

Now do the same with these.

1. She was very .... of our efforts to help.
    (a) **appreciable** (b) **appreciative** (c) **appreciating** (d) **appreciate**

2. The manager said he believed we would win the contract, but I knew that we didn't really stand a / an ....
    (a) **possibility** (b) **probability** (c) **chance** (d) **opportunity**

3. The proposals he put forward were excellent. ...., it quickly became apparent that they would work when put into practice.
    (a) **Moreover** (b) **However** (c) **Nevertheless** (d) **Although**

4. We need to remain .... to the needs of our customers, and react accordingly.
    (a) **sensible** (b) **sensitive** (c) **sensitivity** (d) **sensibility**

5. An .... number of working hours are lost every year because of illness and absenteeism.
    (a) **considerate** (b) **considerable** (c) **consistent** (d) **considered**

6. The new salesman refused to wear a tie on ....
    (a) **principle** (b) **principality** (c) **principal** (d) **principally**

7. Nobody raised any .... when we insisted on opening an hour earlier.
    (a) **criticism** (b) **complaints** (c) **protests** (d) **objections**

8. The museum contains several .... works of Renaissance art, including two paintings by Raphael, one by Dürer, one by Titian, and an early sketch by Tintoretto.
    (a) **worthless** (b) **valueless** (c) **priceless** (d) **useless**

9. Despite the recent economic recovery, many people are still looking for ....
    (a) **work** (b) **job** (c) **profession** (d) **career**

10. The Avicenna Partnership is a .... company with a long and successful sales history.
    (a) **respectable** (b) **respectful** (c) **respecting** (d) **respective**

11. Because of increased operating costs, we have been forced to .... our prices.
    (a) **rise** (b) **raze** (c) **raise** (d) **arise**

12. The bank has said it will be happy to .... us the money provided we have suitable collateral.
    (a) **lend** (b) **borrow** (c) **lease** (d) **rent**

13. When we leave the office tonight, ... me to turn everything off and lock up properly.
    (a) **remembrance** (b) **reminisce** (c) **remember** (d) **remind**

14. Because of the current .... situation, we have been forced to close down several of our city center outlets.
    (a) **economical** (b) **economic** (c) **economize** (d) **economics**

15. Shortly before you hold a meeting, it is a good idea to send everyone in the office a .... outlining the main points to be discussed.
    (a) **notify** (b) **notice** (c) **note** (d) **notification**

Continuing, repeating and starting again

The sentences below all contain a word or phrase in bold referring to *continuing something, repeating something*, or *starting something again*. In some of the sentences, the word has been used correctly. In others, the wrong word has been used.

Identify which sentences are correct and which are wrong. Check (✓) the correct sentences, and replace the words in the wrong sentences with a correct word. You will find these words in the other wrong sentences.

1.　　Despite **repeated** (.....................................) warnings, you have failed to show any improvement in your work or your attitude.

2.　　The production line has been temporarily shut down following a report from the Health and Safety officer, but we hope to **ongoing** (.....................................) production as soon as possible.

3.　　The meeting will break for lunch at half past twelve, and **restart** (.....................................) at two.

4.　　I think that we have talked enough about planning permission for the new office. I would like to **reopen** (.....................................) to the previous subject of overdue payments, if that's all right?

5.　　We like to **continuous** (.....................................) good relations with our customers, and take any complaints very seriously indeed.

6.　　The computer crashed on Monday, then again on Wednesday and once more on Friday. If it keeps giving us **persevere** (.....................................) problems, I suggest we get a new one.

7.　　When you try to call someone on the phone, a regular, repeated tone means that the person you are calling is already on the phone. A / An **maintain** (.....................................) tone means that the number you are trying to call is not available.

8.　　We are worried that work on the new warehouse will **progress** (.....................................) too slowly unless we offer the contractors more incentives.

9.　　We understand that you are supposed to retire next month, but we would be delighted if you would **carry on** (.....................................) working for us after that on a part-time basis.

10.　　The economic climate is very bad at the moment, and we are losing over $10,000 a month as a result, but I suggest we **steady** (.....................................) and hope that recovery comes soon.

11.　　Unfortunately, the latest company report will **persist** (.....................................) the unfounded rumor that we are going to close down some departments.

12.　　The managing director called, and says he wants us to **press on** (.....................................) with the proposed changes to the distribution scheme despite opposition from the marketing department.

13.　　The hotel will be closed for renovations between 15 October and 20 November, but will **revert** (.....................................) in time for the Thanksgiving holiday.

14.　　The directors have said they are delighted with the commitment you have shown the company this year, and hope that you will be able to **perpetuate** (.....................................) the good work.

15. If you **continual** (...) in coming in late and taking unauthorized breaks, we will have no option but to dismiss you from your post.

16. Staff absenteeism is a / an **keep up** (...) problem which we need to resolve as soon as possible.

17. The **constant** (...) noise from the highway outside the office makes it very difficult to concentrate.

18. As long as the negotiations continue to **proceed** (...) well, we hope to sign the contract by the end of the month.

19. Unemployment figures have fallen by about 2% every year for the last ten years. It is hoped that this **resume** (...) decrease will continue.

20. If the government agrees to **pursue** (...) its current policy of reducing taxation, we can afford to invest more in developing our technology.

Exercise 2

Complete these sentences using the most appropriate word or phrase from Exercise 1. In some cases you will need to change the form of the word (for example, from an adjective to an adverb), and in some cases more than one option is possible.

1. We have asked them .... to send us the invoice, but they have ignored us every time.

2. The air conditioning is .... breaking down, usually when it's really hot.

3. Sales figures have been dropping by about 3% a month. If this problem ...., we will have to start making staff cutbacks.

4. Rail services between Albion Creek and Elgin City have been suspended while the track is repaired, but will .... early next week.

5. Learning a language isn't easy. You need to .... if you want to make any real progress.

6. One of the most important things you should do in this line of work is .... a sense of humor, especially when things go wrong.

7. The work on the new airport isn't .... fast enough, and won't be finished in time for the beginning of the tourist season.

8. The presentation ended early because of .... interruptions from the audience.

9. Staff development workshops help our team to develop new and more effective ways of working, but eventually many of them .... to their old ways.

10. Everyone is delighted with the quality of service you provide. .... it ....!

Contracts

Look at paragraphs 1 – 6 in the boxes, and answer the questions that follow them.

1.

> This contract is <u>binding</u>, and we expect all the <u>parts</u> involved (both clients *and* suppliers) to <u>abide by</u> the <u>terms and conditions</u> stated in sections 3a – 37g on pages 14 – 17.

1. One of the <u>underlined</u> words / phrases in the above sentence is wrong. Say which one is wrong, and what it *should* be.

   .... should be ....

2. True or false: A contract which is *binding* is flexible and can be changed at any time.
   True / False

3. Which of these words / expressions could replace *abide by*? <u>Underline</u> your answer:
   (A) choose   (B) agree with   (C) obey   (D) change

2.

> On <u>terminator</u> of this contract, the company will be <u>obliged</u> to return any unused materials to the supplier within 28 days, unless <u>provision</u> has been made for a temporary extension. If any of the rules of the contract are <u>broken</u>, all materials must be returned immediately.

1. One of the <u>underlined</u> words in the above sentence is wrong. Say which one is wrong, and what it *should* be.

   .... should be ....

2. True or false: *Provision* has a similar meaning to *arrangement*.
   True / False

3. Rearrange these letters to make two words which have a similar meaning to *obliged*:
   degabtlio   edequrir

   ....

3.

> The contract was originally <u>verbal</u>, but we've finally managed to get the company to give us something on paper. They say that this contract is <u>un-negotiable</u>, but maybe we can persuade the company to <u>amend</u> some of the details before we sign <u>on the dotted line</u>.

1. One of the <u>underlined</u> words / phrases in the above paragraph is wrong. Say which one is wrong, and what it *should* be.

   .... should be ....

2. True or false: The speaker thinks that it might be possible for small changes to be made to the contract before she signs it.
   True / False

3. Rearrange the letters in **bold** to make four words which have the same meaning as *verbal* in this situation
   rola   kosnep   plidemi   etodnurdso

   ....
   ....

4.

> Swillpot Airline Catering Ltd was <u>sued</u> by Pan-Globe Airways when it was found to be <u>in beach of</u> its contract, specifically that it had failed to <u>comply with</u> clause 27B, which <u>stated</u> that food should be "fit for human consumption".

1. One of the <u>underlined</u> words / phrases in the above sentence is wrong. Say which one is wrong, and what it *should* be.

    .... should be ....

2. Find a word or phrase in paragraphs 1 – 3 on the previous page which has a similar meaning to *comply with* in paragraph 4.

    ....

3. True or false: Pan-Globe Airways is unhappy with Swillpot Airline Catering because it has broken *all* of the contract.
    True / False

5.

> Withers Interiors Ltd has entered into an <u>agreement</u> with Sophos Construction to act as sole providers of quality interior fittings <u>commencing</u> 15 August this year. This is to run for 18 months, with a three month <u>period of notification</u> in the event of <u>cancellation</u> by either side.

1. One of the <u>underlined</u> words phrases in the above sentence is wrong. Say which one is wrong, and what it *should* be.

    .... should be ....

2. Which word in the paragraph is the closest in meaning to the noun *contract*?

    ....

3. True or false: If either Withers Interiors Ltd or Sophos Construction want to end the contract, they must tell the other company three months before they do it.
    True / False

6.

> This contract recognizes the <u>anointment</u> of Mr Alan Wiley as non-executive director to the board of AKL Publishing following the company's <u>amalgamation</u> with Berryhill Books. While Mr Wiley may continue to buy stocks in the company, he may not acquire a <u>controlling interest</u>, and he may have no professional dealings with any <u>third parties</u> during this period.

1. One of the <u>underlined</u> words / phrases in the above sentence is wrong. Say which one is wrong, and what it *should* be.

    .... should be ....

2. True or false: AKL Publishing recently separated from Berryhill Books.
    True / False

3. True or false: Mr Wiley can buy as many shares as he likes in the company.
    True / False

4. In addition to sitting on the board of AKL Publishing, how many other companies can Mr Wiley work for?

    ....

Different situations

Look at situations 1 – 10, and answer the question that follows each one.

1.

If it is formal, it should begin with a polite salutation. If you don't know the recipient's name, call them *Sir* or *Madam*, but if you know their name, always use it (beginning with *Mr* for men and *Ms* for women). It should be brief, clear and to the point. End with *Yours sincerely* if you know the recipient's name, or *Yours faithfully* if you don't. Some people end theirs with *Yours truly*. Only use *Best wishes* at the end if it is informal.

- What is the speaker talking about? ....

2.

Mr Jenkins: What's the schedule for today?
Ms Ranscombe: Well, after everyone has arrived and registered, there will be coffee in the reception area. This will give everyone a chance to meet their fellow delegates and do some networking. This will be followed by a plenary session in the main hall: I believe the speaker will be giving a presentation on new marketing trends. After a break at 11 o'clock there will be different seminars for areas of special interest. The afternoon will consist of a series of workshops, and then there will be an evening reception and dinner for all the participants.

- Where are Mr Jenkins and Ms Ranscombe? ....

3.

Ms Akkabar: Hello, Mr Andrews. What can I do for you today?
Mr Andrews: I originally just wanted a check-up, but two days ago I lost a filling, and I think one of my crowns is coming loose. I guess that will be expensive to fix.
Ms Akkabar: Well, it might be, but we have various payment options that might spread the cost. Take a seat and I'll have a look. Hmm. Your gums look a bit sore. How often do you brush and floss?
Mr Andrews: About five times a day!

- What is Ms Akkabar's job? ....

4.

The company is committed to helping employees learn more about their jobs and develop their skills, so we run regular sessions to facilitate this. These are usually in the form of seminars and workshops, and cover a wide range of subjects, including leadership skills, problem solving, decision making, negotiation skills and interpersonal development. Our employees can then revise and practice these skills through our on line program which is run on the company intranet.

- What is the speaker talking about? ....

5.

Hello? Is that Amanda Mellors? Oh, well, could you put me through then? You can't get through? Oh, her line is engaged. I see. No, I can't hang on, I'm afraid. Could you give me her extension? It's confidential, is it? Well, could you ask her to get back to me later? Hello? HELLO? I don't believe it, I've been cut off.

- What is the speaker doing? ....

6.

Each employee has at least one of these a year. Each session lasts about 45 minutes, and we ask them various questions. For example, we ask them if they think the work they are doing meets the correct standards and whether or not they have met the objectives we have set for them. We also like to know if they are happy with the way their career is progressing, if they would like to do something more challenging, and also if they receive sufficient encouragement, praise and motivation from their managers.

▪ Rearrange the letters in **bold** to make words: The speaker is talking about his company's **fatfs spapialar** program. ....

7.

Andy: My new boss is abrasive, bigoted, conceited, confrontational, critical, insensitive, intolerant and obstinate.
Maureen: You two have a lot in common, then.

▪ Does Andy have a good boss or a bad one? ....

8.

Ms Collins: You will be expected to oversee the work of the production department, agree product specifications with sales departments and time schedules with the stock control department, ensure the product is manufactured according to agreed specifications, inspect the quality of the finished product, produce sales reports for the head office, visit and negotiate with suppliers on base material prices and deal with everyday problems as they arise.
Mr Sheppard: Anything else?
Ms Collins: Yes. Make my coffee. Two sugars and plenty of cream, please.

▪ What is Ms Collins explaining to Mr Sheppard? ....

9.

Ms Colley: What's your diagnosis? Is it serious?
Mr Sagala: Oh no. You have a throat infection, but it's fairly minor and nothing to worry about.
Ms Colley: Can you treat it?
Mr Sagala: Oh yes, I'll give you a prescription for antibiotics. They should cure it. But make an appointment to come back and see me in a week. It's slightly contagious, so I suggest you take a few days off work. I'll write you a sick note.

▪ How does Mr Sagala make his living? ....

10.

Mr Samson: It says here that we owe them $180, but the order was only for $131.
Ms Grant: Yes, but that price was exclusive of tax.
Mr Samson: I know, but even with tax it should only come to $165.
Ms Grant: That's true. Oh, hang on, look what it says at the bottom. Package and delivery: $15.
Mr Samson: Oh, right. Well, I guess we had better pay them. Who do we make the remittance payable to?
Ms Grant: Oh, we don't need to send them anything. The payment will be automatically deducted from our account at the end of the month. Unfortunately, what this doesn't show us is the import duty we will have to pay. I guess we can expect to get a bill from Customs soon.

▪ What are Mr Samson and Ms Grant looking at? ....

Look at the situations again, and highlight the key words and expressions that helped you to identify what each one is about.

Earnings, rewards and benefits

Exercise 1
Complete the first part of each word in **bold** in the sentences with the second part in the box.

-an	-ance	-ary	-ble	-ction	-ement	-eration	-ge	-hting	-imum
-ise	-kage	-lement	-me	-nus	-roll	-sion	-slip	-time	-ve

1. A *wage* is money that is normally paid to an employee on a weekly basis, and a **sal**........................ .... is money that is usually paid to an employee on a monthly or yearly basis.

2. **Remun**................................... is the formal word for money that an employee receives for doing his / her job.

3. When we work for more than the normal working time, we say that we work (and therefore earn) **over**.................................... .

4. An automatic and regular increase in pay is called an **incr**.................................... .

5. Money that is removed from our earnings to pay for tax etc, is called a **dedu**.................................... .

6. The **min**.................................... **wa**.................................... is the lowest hourly wage which a company can legally pay its employees.

7. Time for which work is paid at twice the normal rate (for example, on national holidays) is called **dou**.................................... **ti**.................................... .

8. A **pen**.................................... **pl**.................................... helps people to save money for when they retire from work.

9. When you want more money for the work you do, you might ask your boss for a **ra**.................................... .

10. If an employee needs some of his / her wages paid before the usual pay day, he / she might ask for an **adv**.................................... .

11. A **pay**.................................... shows an employee how much pay he / she has received, and how much has been removed for tax, insurance, etc.

12. An extra payment made in addition to a normal payment (sometimes received by sales people for selling more than their quota) is called a **bo**.................................... .

13. A **pay**.......... is the list a company keeps that shows all the people employed and paid by that company.

14. A rewards **pac**.................................... is the money and other benefits offered with a job.

15. A **weig**.................................... is an additional amount of money paid to an employee to compensate him / her for living in an expensive area.

16. By law, American companies have to give their employees the right to take paid vacations: this is known as **lea**.................................... **entit**.................................... .

Exercise 2

Now do the same with these.

-ance   -ans   -ated   -ation   -ay   -count   -dancy   -den   -dex   -diture
-ensurate   -et   -faction   -fit   -ission   -ked   -ock   -ome   -ormance
-oss   -ring   -shake   -te   -tions   -tive

1. **Inc**..................................... is another word for the money that people receive for working. The money that they spend is known as **expen**..................................... .

2. For some people, the money that they earn for doing a job is less important than job **satis**..................................... (the pleasure they get from doing their job).

3. A sales person usually earns a percentage of the sales value of the product or service he / she sells: this is called a **comm**..................................... .

4. Some companies offer their employees **st**..................................... **op**..................................... which means that the employees can buy stocks at a price lower than the normal price.

5. Some companies have **incen**..................................... **pl**..................................... where they offer their employees extra rewards and benefits for good attendance, increased productivity, etc.

6. The amount of money an employee receives each hour, day, week, etc, is known as an hourly / daily / weekly **ra**..................................... .

7. If an employee loses his / her job because the company doesn't need or can't afford to keep him / her, they might receive **redun**..................................... **p**..................................... .

8. Some companies offer their employees a **dis**..................................... on the product and services they sell, which means that the employee can buy them for less than the usual price.

9. If an employee takes a job in another place which is a long way from his / her original home and place of work, he / she might be offered a **reloc**..................................... **allow**..................................... .

10. Some companies have a policy of **pro**..................................... **sha**....................................., where some or all of the money that they make is given to their employees.

11. **Gr**..................................... is an adjective used to describe an employee's earnings before tax, national insurance, etc, has been removed.

12. **N**..................................... is an adjective used to describe an employee's earnings after tax, national insurance, etc, has been removed.

13. When the money that an employee receives rises automatically by the percentage increase in the cost of living, we say that it is **in**.....................................**-lin**..................................... .

14. If the amount of money an employee receives depends on how well he / she does his / her job, we say that it is **perf**..................................... **rel**..................................... .

15. When the money that an employee earns is based on age, experience, qualifications, position in the company, etc, we say that it is **comm**..................................... .

16. When an employee leaves his / her job after a long period with the company, he / she might be offered a large amount of money known as a **gol**..................................... **hand**..................................... .

Entertainment, art, sport and the media

Complete paragraphs A – H with words from the boxes, and decide what the speaker is talking about in each case. In some cases, more than one answer may be possible.

(A)

articles	circulation	coverage	current	editor	events	features
journalists	lively	objective	Press	readership	researched	

After a very successful year in which they had the country's highest (1) ...., their
(2) .... has dropped recently. This has come as a major surprise, as their
(3) .... of major national and world (4) .... is excellent,
their (5) .... and (6) .... are well-(7) ....
...... and they approach (8) .... affairs in a way that is (9) ....
but (10) .... and interesting. Did you know that the (11) ....
and some of her (12) .... recently won a National (13) ....
Club award?

(B)

anchor	break	broadcasting	complaints	live	network	off-screen
	on air	reporter	studio	technical		

There was clearly some sort of (1) .... problem in the (2) .... You
could see the (3) .... on the screen talking to the viewers, but you couldn't hear a
word she was saying. However, you *could* hear the (4) ...., who obviously didn't
realize that even though he was (5) .... (and so out of sight of the viewers), he was
still (6) ...., and his voice was going out (7) .... across the
entire (8) .... You wouldn't have believed the language he was using: I bet there
were a few angry (9) .... from viewers to the (10) .... standards
committee after that! It was so funny that I was really disappointed when they cut to a commercial
(11) ....

(C)

action	anthology	biographical	character	copy	issued	Literature
	plot	recommend	set	works	writer	

This is one of the most famous (1) .... by the American (2) ....
Ernest Hemingway, and one for which he won the Nobel Prize for (3) .... What I like
about it is the simple (4) ...., and the fact that the main (5) .... is
a simple, everyday man fighting the forces of nature. The story is (6) .... in Cuba, and
the (7) .... takes place mainly at sea. It's semi-(8) ...., as the
old man in the story really existed. I would (9) .... it very much. It has recently been
re (10) .... in an (11) .... of the man's greatest works: I
suggest you pick up a (12) .... as soon as you can.

(D)

actors	Award	box-office	cinematography	critics	director
	effects	performances	release	scenery	soundtrack

I'm not particularly keen on the (1) ....'s style, but his latest offering is excellent and
is bound to be a major (2) .... success. I wouldn't even be surprised if it picked up
an Academy (3) .... or two (or three or four). Apart from the (4) ...., who all
give excellent (5) ...., the special (6) .... are excellent,
the (7) .... is beautiful, the (8) .... is very impressive, and
there is a lively (9) .... When it finished, even cynical (10) ....
such as myself got to our feet and applauded. You should go and see it as soon as it is on
general (11) ....

(E)

audience	auditorium	backers	cast	curtain	dialog	half	lights
lines	opening	performance	rehearsed	scenery	scriptwriter	stage	

Last night was the (1) .... night, and from what I could see, many in the
(2) .... were probably hoping it would be the last. By the time the (3) ....
had opened and the (4) .... had come up on the (5) .... for
the second (6) .... of the (7) ...., the (8) ....
was half empty. The (9) .... clearly hadn't (10) .... enough and
kept forgetting their (11) ...., the (12) .... could have been
written by a ten-year-old child, and the (13) .... looked like it would collapse if there
was a strong wind. The poor (14) .... were probably in tears at the money they would
be losing, and if the (15) .... never worked in professional theater again, I doubt
anyone would be sorry.

(F)

accomplished	acquired	Admission	ancient	art	artists	collection
collector	contribution	exhibitions	exhibits	galleries	portraits	

There are 20 (1) .... containing a total of over 50,000 (2) ....,
of which about 3,000 come from (3) .... Egypt, and which were (4) ....
from a private (5) .... in the 1950s. There is also an excellent section on modern
(6)..., which has a permanent (7) .... of landscapes,
(8) ...., sculptures, and still lifes by some of the 20th century's most (9) ....
and significant (10) .... There are regular temporary (11) ....
as well. (12) .... is free for everyone, although visitors are encouraged to make a
voluntary (13) .... of $10 to help pay for the upkeep.

(G)

astute	band	compilation	crowd	fans	groups	hits	note
recordings	repertoire	singer	studio	track	variations		

I am not particularly keen on live (1) .... and I usually avoid heavy-metal rock
(2) .... like *The Würst*, but this is different. From the opening (3) ....
on the first (4) ...., to the last cheers of the (5) .... as they
worship their leather-clad heroes, you feel that you are right there in the front row as the
(6) .... goes through its (7) .... of number 1 (8) ....
The sound is crystal-clear throughout, and there are some interesting (9) ....
on the usual (10) .... versions (including an acoustic version of "Did You Eat My
Hamster?'). Between the songs, there are also some (11) .... and witty comments
to the (12) .... from lead (13) .... and guitarist Oswald
Gutt. If you like this, you should also check out their latest (14) ...., "*The Very Best
of The Würst*', which contains 16 of their most famous numbers from the last 15 years.

(H)

beat	captains	cheerleaders	coaches	draw	encouragement	opponents
pitch	referee	score	spectators	stadium	supporters	teams	triumph	win

The (1) .... in the (2) .... cheered and clapped as the two
(3) .... came onto the (4) .... Who would (5) ....
the event this year? Would the Denver Deadbeats (6) .... again? Or would it be the
Washington Wasters time to (7) .... their deadliest (8) .... at
last? The two (9) .... shook hands, the (10) .... tossed a coin,
and it was game on! The (11) .... in their shiny red costumes went through their
well-practiced routine, the (12) .... sang and chanted slogans, and the (13) ....
nervously paced the sidelines, shouting advice and (14) .... The final
(15) ....was a (16) .... at four goals each.

Food and eating out

Test your knowledge with this vocabulary quiz.

1. Look at this formal notice printed at the bottom of a menu. Replace the formal words and expressions in **bold** with less formal words. (1 point each. Total: 6 points)

    Patrons are *requested* to *refrain from* smoking in the *dining area*. If they *wish* to smoke, they should *retire* to the bar.

    (a) .... are (b) ....

    (c) .... to smoke in the (d) .... If they

    (e) .... to smoke, they should (f) ....

    to the bar.

2. This extract from an article on healthy eating contains two <u>factual</u> mistakes. Can you identify the two words that are responsible for causing these mistakes (2 points) and correct them (2 points)? (Total: 4 points)

    Wholesome food should always be rich in vitamins and minerals, have a minimum amount of sugar and salt, be free from preservatives and other artificial ingredients, and be high in cholesterol. The best way of preparing meat and vegetables is to fry them, as this helps them to retain all their goodness.

    The wrong words in the extract are .... and ....

    The words *should* be .... and ....

3. Find words or expressions in the extract in number 2 above that are closest in meaning to:

    (a) *the part or parts of a food that are healthy for you* ....

    (b) *the different things that are needed to make a meal* ....

    (c) *containing a lot of something (2 possible answers)* ....

    (d) *very small* ....

    (e) *keep* ....

    (f) *healthy* ....

    (g) *cooking* ....

    (h) *lacking / not having* ....

    (i) *not real / not genuine* ....

    (j) *method* ....

    (1 point each. Total: 10 points)

4. Complete these sentences with an appropriate preposition or particle.
    (1 point for each preposition / particle or combination. Total: 6 points)

    (a) *I can't eat nuts because I'm allergic* .... *them.*

    (b) *He's not keen* .... *Asian food in general, but he is very fond*
    .... *Japanese food, especially sushi.*

    (c) *My doctor has advised me to cut* ....
    my salt intake, and cut .... *meat from my diet altogether. He's also*
    suggested I give .... *candy and other sugary foods.*

5.   This extract from an article on food contains <u>five</u> wrong words. Can you find them and correct them? (1 point each. Total: 5 points)

More consumers these days are interested in where their food comes from. As a result, there is now much more demand for things like free ranger eggs, and organism fruit, vegetables and meat. People are also more concerned about artificial additions and colorings in their food, and of course everyone is worried about the potential dangers of genetically modification (GM) food. As a result, fat food outlets are beginning to lose customers.

The wrong words in the extract are ...., ..., .

...., ... and ....

The words should be ...., ...,

...., ... and ....

6.   Rearrange the letters in **bold** to make words and expressions (1 point each. Total: 14 points)

*I really would not **meordcenm** the new restaurant on Sebastopol Street. Last week I made a **sioenervrat** for dinner, but when we arrived at the restaurant, our table wasn't ready. When we eventually sat down, the **everisc** was slow and the **nagwiti** staff were rude. When the food eventually arrived, the **rotniops** were tiny (all right if you are on a **tide**, but not so good if you're feeling hungry). My chicken was **rudecodnoke** (in fact it was still red on the inside!), and my partner's steak, which she wanted **earr**, was so **lewl-neod** that it was almost **trunb**! When the **kcech** arrived at the end of the meal, we discovered that we had been **hogvdeacrer** by almost $20. We refused to pay the 10% **evsirec ragceh**, and naturally we didn't leave a **pit**.*

(a) meordcenm = ...

(b) sioenervrat = ...

(c) everisc = ...

(d) nagwiti = ...

(e) rotniops = ...

(f) tide = ...

(g) rudecodnoke = ...

(h) earr = ...

(i) lewl-neod = ...

(j) trunb = ...

(k) kcech = ...

(l) hogvdeacrer = ...

(m) evsirec ragceh = ...

(n) pit = ...

Hotels

Exercise 1

Look at this extract from a hotel information leaflet and complete the gaps with words or phrases from the box. You must use one word twice.

all-inclusive (AI)	amenities	bed and breakfast (B+B)		business and conference
double	en suite	facilities	family	full-board half-board Internet
non-residents	occupancy	options	pay-to-view	pool quote rates residents
room service	safety deposit	self-catering	single	suite supplement twin

---

The Five Pillars Hotel and Resort

The following room (1) .... apply from April to October
(prices are per person per night):

- (2) .... room (1 single bed): $50
- (3) .... room (2 single beds): $35
- (4) .... room (1 king size bed): $35 (+ single person
(5) .... (6) .... of $20)
- (7) .... room (1 king size bed, 2 single beds): $35 (adults)
$20 (children)
- (8) .... (bedroom, separate living room,
bathroom): $65
All rooms are (9) .... (attached bathroom with bath,
shower and WC)

Special group (10) .... are available for groups of
15 or more. Call us for a (11) .... (the number is at the
bottom of this page)

Room (12) .... include:
- Minibar. • (13) .... box. • Tea and coffee making
facilities. • (14) .... satellite TV.
- Wi-Fi (15) .... connection.

Hotel (16) .... include:
- Restaurant and bar (open to (17) .... and
(18) ....).
- 24-hour (19) .... (light meals only between
11.30 pm and 6.00 am) • Heated outdoor (20) ....
- (21) .... center.

The following meal-plan (22) .... are available:
- (23) .... (*European Plan*: room only, no meals included)
- (24) .... (*Bermuda Plan*: includes room + morning meal)
- (25) .... (*Modified American Plan*: includes room,
morning + evening meals)
- (26) .... (*American Plan*: includes room + all meals)
- (27) .... (Includes room, all meals, snacks, tea, coffee
and other drinks)

Now do the same with the next part of the information leaflet. Again, you will need to use one word twice.

---

advance   cashiers   chain   chambermaids   charged   check-in   check-out
chefs   competitive   email   experience   guests   housekeeping   peak period
receptionists   reservations   shuttle   staff   training   transfer   uniform
vacancies   vacated   waiters   waitresses   Web site

Please note that the hotel is very busy during our (1) ....
between June and August, so (2) ....
(3) .... are essential. We recommend that at other times you
telephone first to see if there are any (4) .... Alternatively,
(5) .... us at info@fivepillarshotel.com.

Also please note that the earliest (6) .... time is
2.00 pm, and the latest (7) .... time is 11.30 am.
All rooms must be (8) .... by this time, or
(9) .... will be (10) .... for
an extra night.

If you are arriving or leaving by air, the hotel operates an airport bus
(11) .... service. (12) .... time
from the airport to the hotel is approximately 40 minutes. This service is free to all our (13)
....

The Five Pillars Hotel is part of the *Elite* (14) ....,
with over 75 hotels and motels throughout the USA and Canada. Call 0119 ELITEYU for
more information, or visit our (15) ....
at www.luvelite.com.

JOBS ✳ JOBS ✳ JOBS ✳ JOBS ✳ JOBS

Are you interested in working for any of the Elite hotels? We are always looking for new
(16) .... Here are just a few of the areas you could work
in. No previous (17) .... is necessary, as full (18) ....
.... will be given. We will offer you a
(19) .... salary and provide you with a free
(20) .... Contact us on the number above.

▪ Cleaners and (21) .... to work in our busy
(22) .... departments.
▪ (23) .... to meet and greet our customers when they arrive.
▪ (24) .... and (25) .... to
serve in our popular restaurants and bars.
▪ (26) .... to prepare quality meals in our kitchens.
▪ (27) .... to run our exchange bureaus and handle the
financial side of the business.

Job advertising

Exercise 1

Match the words and phrases in the box with the dictionary definitions 1 – 24.

advance	application	basic salary	benefits	candidate	colleagues
commencing	commission	cover letter	drive (*noun*)	experience	incentive
increment	interview	leading (*adjective*)	motivate	post	qualified
relocation allowance	responsibilities	résumé	rewards package	team	vacancy

1.   To have the right qualifications. ....
2.   Money which is given to a sales person for selling a certain amount of goods (usually expressed as a percentage of the value of goods sold). ....
3.   To encourage somebody to do something. ....
4.   Something which encourages you to work harder. ....
5.   The different things you need to do as part of your job. ....
6.   A letter that you send with a résumé, document, etc, which gives basic information about why you are sending it. ....
7.   (In a job) To reach a higher position with more money and more responsibility.
        ....
8.   The collection of different things that you receive in return for doing your job. ....
        ....
9.   The people you work with in a company. ....
10.   A formal word for a job. ....
11.   A detailed list of your qualifications, work experience, etc. ....
12.   The knowledge and skills that you get by doing a particular job. ....
13.   A job in a company which is currently not filled by anybody. ....
14.   The things that you get for doing your job in addition to money. ....
15.   The minimum amount of money you receive for doing a job. ....
16.   A group of people who work together in one company or department.
        ....
17.   The questioning of a person who is applying for a job. ....
18.   Money which is sometimes paid to somebody when they leave one place to go and work in another place. ....
19.   A formal request (usually written) for a job. ....
20.   A more formal word for beginning or starting. ....
21.   A word describing a very successful or important company. ....
22.   A regular pay rise, often based on how well an employee performs at work.
        ....
23.   A quality you probably have if you are an energetic and enthusiastic worker.
        ....
24.   A person who applies for a job. ....

Exercise 2

Look at this conversation and complete the gaps with words or expressions from Exercise 1. Try to do this *without* looking back at exercise 1.

Bob: Hi Terry. What are you reading?

Terry: The jobs pages in the paper.

Bob: Oh really? Anything interesting?

Terry: Well, there's something here I like the sound of. Modus International, a
         (1) .... supplier of auto parts, has a (2) ....
         for the (3) .... of Sales Manager in its Seattle office.

Bob: That sounds like your kind of job. When does it begin?

Terry: Let me see. Er, (4) .... April 1st, it says here. That's in three weeks' time.

Bob: You'd better get your (5) .... in, if you're interested. What else does it say about the job?

Terry: It says that the successful (6) .... should be suitably
(7) .... and should have had extensive (8) ....
in sales management.

Bob: That sounds perfect. You've got a university degree in business management, and you've been working in sales for more than five years.

Terry: I guess so. It also says that he or she should be able to work as part of a
(9) ...., and should have (10) .... and the
ability to (11) .... and inspire his or her (12) ....

Bob: Well, that's great! You've always got on with the people you work with, and everyone is always saying how you're able to encourage people to work harder.

Terry: That's true. It also says that the (13) .... include liaising with colleagues around the country, training new staff and presenting a full report to the board of directors twice a year.

Bob: It all sounds quite good. What's the company offering in return?

Terry: The (14) .... they're offering looks very attractive. It includes a
(15) .... of $40,000 per annum...

Bob: What does that mean?

Terry: Well, that's the minimum amount of money that you can earn during the year. In addition to that, they're offering 10% (16) .... on all sales made.

Bob: Well, that's a good (17) .... The more you work, the more you sell. And the more you sell, the more money you'll make!

Terry: Exactly. There's also a guaranteed annual (18) .... of $2,500, and a
(19) .... of $4,000.

Bob: What's that for?

Terry: To pay me for moving to the area, finding an apartment, and so on. Oh, and there are other
(20) ...., such as a company car, free medical and dental insurance and free meals in the cafeteria. It also says that there is room to (21) ....,
so I might end up with an even better job within the company.

Bob: So what should you do if you're interested in applying for the job?

Terry: It says I should send my (22) .... together with a
(23) ...., to their head office in Los Angeles. If the company is
interested, they'll contact me to arrange an (24) .... at one of their
offices nearer home.

Bob: Go for it! I can come and visit you. I've always wanted to see the Pacific Ocean!

Also see *Contracts* on pages 12 and 13, *Earnings, rewards and benefits* on pages 16 and 17, and *Job recruitment* on pages 26 and 27.

Job recruitment

Exercise 1
Look at the pairs of words and phrases in **bold** in this article, and decide which one is best in each situation. In several cases, *both* words are correct.

Part 1

When a company has a (1) **vacancy / vacant** for a job, and it needs to (2) **hire / recruit** a new member of (3) **crew / staff**, it usually (4) **publicizes / advertises** the (5) **post / position**. It either does this (6) **internally / internationally** (for example, in the company magazine or on a company noticeboard, so that the job is only open to people already working for the company), or (7) **extensively / externally** in the "situations vacant" section of a newspaper. It might also use a recruitment (8) **agency / agenda**, which helps people to find (9) **job / work**.

A job advertisement has to give an accurate (10) **describing / description** of the job and what the company needs and expects from the (11) **applicant / application** (the person who is (12) **applying / appalling** for the job). These (13) **requirements / requisitions** might include (14) **qualifications / qualities** (academic, vocational or professional), (15) **experience / experiences** in similar lines of work, and personal (16) **qualifications / qualities** (for example, it might say that you need to be (17) **practicing / practical**, (18) **professional / professorial** and have a sense of humor).

Most advertisements specify the (19) **rewards / remuneration** that the company can offer in return for your work (including the basic annual (20) **wage / salary**, any commission you could receive, regular pay (21) **raises / increments**, and so on). Some advertisements will also tell you about other (22) **benefits / beneficial** (including paid annual (23) **leave / vacations**, free medical care, a company car, free meals in the cafeteria, etc) that you might receive. If the (24) **packet / package** they are offering is very generous and attractive, and is (25) **commensurate/ commendable** with the work that is necessary, the company can expect a lot of people to apply for the job.

Part 2

If somebody is interested in the job, they are usually asked to send to send their (1) **CV / résumé** with a (2) **cover / covering** letter. Alternatively, they might be asked to (3) **fill in / fill out** an (4) **application / applicant** form and (5) **submit / send** it to the company. The managers of the company will read these and then make a (6) **short list / small list** of the people it wants to (7) **attend / attempt** an interview. At the same time, it will (8) **reject / turn down** those who it feels are (9) **unsuitable / unthinkable**.

During and after the interviews, the managers will consider the different aspects of the (10) **candidates / applicants** to decide whether they have the correct (11) **potency / potential** for the job. These might include physical (12) **apparition / appearance** (are they smart and well presented?), general (13) **disposition / disposal** (for example, are they friendly and easy to work with?), special (14) **skills / abilities** (for example, are they computer literate, can they drive, or do they speak any other languages?) and (15) **interests / hobbies** (what do they like doing in their free time?). They might also consider their family (16) **backing / background** (are they married, do they have children?) and (17) **medicine / medical** history. The person who most closely (18) **suits / matches** the (19) **profile / criteria** decided by the managers will then be accepted for the job.

Before somebody is (20) **offered / suggested** the job, s/he is asked to provide (21) **referees / references** from people who know him / her (usually a former (22) **employer / employee**, a (23) **colleague / co-worker**, and / or a close friend). Before s/he actually starts working, s/he may go through an (24) **induction / introduction** program to learn more about the company and the job. Sometimes, s/he may be given a (25) **temporary / temporal** contract and obliged to complete a (26) **trial / probationary** period (where his / her employers make sure that s/he is suitable for the job) before being offered something that is more (27) **permanence / permanent** (a *fixed-term* or *open-ended* contract, for example). After s/he has been with the company for a while, there will probably be an (28) **appraisal / appreciable**, to assess how s/he is getting on. These may be repeated on a regular basis throughout his / her time with the company.

Exercise 2

Complete the passages below with appropriate words or phrases from Exercise 1. You will need to change the form of some of the words.

1. I've got all the right (a) .... for the (b) ....
    I saw being (c) .... in our local paper, including a Diploma in Business
    Studies. Unfortunately, I don't have any (d) .... In fact, I've never even
    worked before! I imagine the company will fill the post (e) .... anyway,
    as they probably already have the right people for the job on site.

2. The job (a) .... in this newspaper (b) ....
    is rather vague. It says what the job is, but it doesn't give any information about
    (c) .... (I'm not going to (d) ....
    for a job if I don't know how much I'm going to earn), and it doesn't say what sort of
    (e) .... it is looking for in the successful
    (f) ....

3. I asked my boss for a (a) .... but she said that I needed to work harder
    if I wanted more money. She also said I needed to be more (b) ....
    in my approach to my work. I get the impression that she thinks I'm completely
    (c) .... for the work I do. This isn't good news, as I'm still on my
    (d) .... period, and I'm worried that when that period is up, I'll be asked
    to move on. Just to be prepared, I'm keeping an eye out for (e) ....
    elsewhere. I've already got my (f) .... printed out and ready to send off
    when the time comes. Unfortunately, I doubt I'll get a good (g) ....
    from my boss!

Also see *Contracts* on pages 12 and 13, *Earnings, rewards and benefits* on pages 16 and 17, and *Job advertising* on pages 24 and 25.

Location and direction

Where is the **movie theater** on the map on the next page? Work it out by reading sentences 1 – 26 below, and matching the roads, buildings and other places mentioned with the letters (A, B, C, etc) on the map. The movie theater is not actually mentioned in any of the sentences, so you will have to use deduction and a process of elimination to find it. The sentences are in no particular order.

1. Stallone Street runs alongside the railway line.

2. Clemenceau Avenue connects Dominion Street with Central Avenue.

3. Easy Street is a one-way street.

4. Central Avenue runs through the middle of the town, parallel to Dominion Street.

5. City Hall faces Washington Park.

6. If you want to get to the library from City Hall, the best way is to cross Dominion Street, walk through Washington Park to Central Avenue, and walk west along Central Avenue until you get to Commercial Street. You'll find the library at the far end of Commercial Street.

7. To get to the department store from the library, cross over Commercial Street and walk towards Central Avenue. You'll see the department store on your left.

8. There is a deli on the corner of Central Avenue and Telegraph Road.

9. You cannot drive your car along Commercial Street: it is a pedestrian-only zone.

10. The post office is at the intersection of Commercial Street and Central Avenue.

11. The nightclub is next to the fast food restaurant.

12. There is a tourist information office on the corner of Stallone Street and Telegraph Road, directly opposite the station.

13. Washington Park is surrounded on all four sides by roads.

14. The bus station is on the corner of Stallone Street and Telegraph Road, directly across the road from the tourist information office.

15. The railway station is in the south-east of the town.

16. To get to the Grand Hotel from the station, the best way is to cross Stallone Street, walk along Telegraph Road and at the end of the road turn left onto Central Avenue. Take the second road on your right, and you'll find the hotel at the far end of this road.

17. The safest way to get to Washington Park from the art gallery is to use the pedestrian underpass that goes under Clemenceau Avenue.

18. Park Lane is at right angles to Central Avenue and Dominion Street.

19. The fast food restaurant is at the end of Dominion Street, where it meets Easy Street and Park Lane.

20. The nightclub is on Park Lane.

21. Commercial Street and Telegraph Road are parallel to each other, but at opposite ends of the town.

22. The museum is adjacent to the post office.

23. The shopping mall is to the west of City Hall, just past Marlene's bar.

24. To get from the bus station to Luigi's restaurant, go along Telegraph Road, and turn left at the intersection. The restaurant is the first building on your left.

25. The Grand Hotel is diagonally across Dominion Street from City Hall.

26. Marlene's bar is between City Hall and the shopping mall.

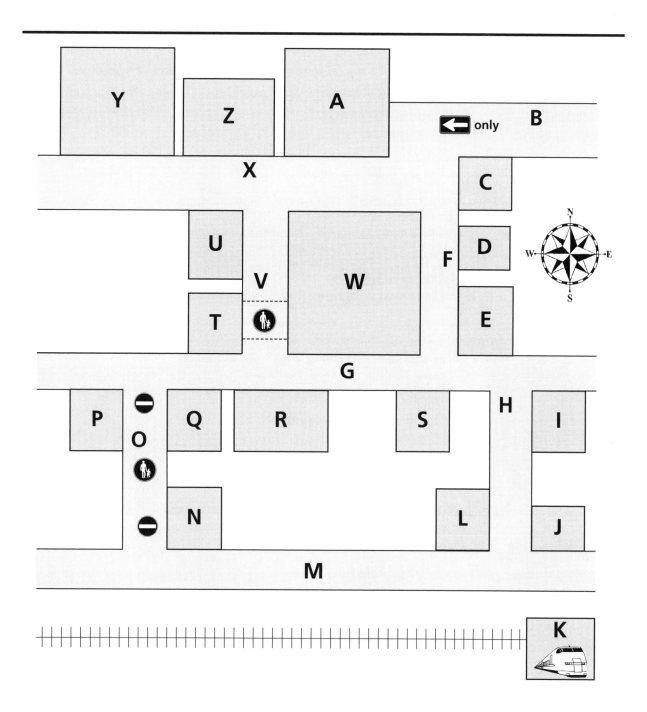

A = ...	B = ...	C = ...	D = ...
E = ...	F = ...	G = Central Avenue	H = ...
I = ...	J = ...	K = ...	L = ...
M = ...	N = ...	O = ...	P = ...
Q = ...	R = ...	S = ...	T = ...
U = ...	V = ...	W = ...	X = ...
Y = ...	Z = ...		

Look at sentences 1 – 26 again, and <u>underline</u> or <mark>highlight</mark> the key words and expressions of *location* and *direction* that helped you to navigate your way around the map. Make a note of these words and expressions, and try to make them an active part of your vocabulary.

Linking ideas

If you take the TOEIC® Test of Spoken English, you might be asked to give a recommendation, state your opinion about something, or describe the cause and / or effect of something. Your language will flow more naturally and your ideas will be clearer if you are able to "join" your ideas together using conjunctions such as *and*, so, *because*, *but*, etc, and other expressions.

Each of the paragraphs below contains a gap. This gap can be completed with one *or more* of the words or phrases below each paragraph. Decide which of them can be used.

1. Visitors to another country should respect the local environment. ....
   they should respect the local customs.
   (A) **Therefore**   (B) **Likewise**   (C) **Similarly**   (D) **In the same way**

2. .... bringing much-needed money to developing countries, tourism
   provides employment for the local population.
   (A) **Besides**   (B) **In the same way**   (C) **As well as**   (D) **In addition to**

3. Tourism brings much-needed money to developing countries. ....,
   it provides employment for the local population.
   (A) **Furthermore**   (B) **In addition**   (C) **Along with**   (D) **Moreover**

4. The company lost a large share of its market to a competitor. ....,
   it had to close down two of its factories.
   (A) **Consequently**   (B) **Likewise**   (C) **Because of**   (D) **As a result**

5. The acting in the movie was terrible, the story was boring and the sound quality was very poor.
   ...., I would not recommend it to anyone.
   (A) **In brief**   (B) **So**   (C) **In the same way**   (D) **Correspondingly**

6. When we made a loss for the third year in a row, two hundred factory workers lost their jobs
   .... half the sales department.
   (A) **together**   (B) **also**   (C) **along with**   (D) **similarly**

7. During the war, many young men went abroad to fight. ....,
   the birth rate dropped sharply during and after this period.
   (A) **For this reason**   (B) **Consequently**   (C) **Besides**   (D) **Since**

8. Economic activity in the area has declined .... poor government
   investment.
   (A) **because of**   (B) **due to**   (C) **as a result of**   (D) **on account of**

9. .... my home town is mainly industrial, there is very little reason for
   tourists to visit it.
   (A) **Thanks to**   (B) **Because of**   (C) **Owing to**   (D) **Seeing as**

10. "The Clockwork Gallery" toy museum is not only popular with children: it is popular with adults
    ....
    (A) **as well**   (B) **too**   (C) **also**   (D) **in addition**

11. .... offering a generous salary and other benefits, the company
    received very few applications for the job.
    (A) **In spite of**   (B) **However**   (C) **Despite**   (D) **Nevertheless**

12. There is only one hotel in the town and it is always full. ...., if you
    want a room there, you should book well in advance.
    (A) **Therefore**   (B) **However**   (C) **Due to**   (D) **Consequently**

Meetings and presentations

Look at this opening address from a company's annual general meeting (AGM) and fill in the gaps with words and phrases from the box. The first letter of each word has been removed from the box and put into the opening address.

```
-articipants    -atters    -bjectives    -chedule    -chieve    -ddress
    -ecommendations    -elcoming    -eport    -et through    -genda    -hair
-inutes    -larification    -loor    -loses    -nterrupt    -oals    -oints    -omplaints
    -ontribute    -otes    -pen    -pen floor    -pinions    -ringing up    -riority
        -rogress    -ssues    -ttendance    -uestions    -ummarizing    -upporting
```

Mr Roberts: Good morning everyone.

Participants: Good morning.

Mr Roberts: I'd like to (1) o.. this, our tenth annual general meeting,
                 by (2) w.. you all. It's good to see so many
                 (3) p.. here today – in fact, this is probably the best
                 (4) a.. we've had at a meeting for a long time – and I'd
                 like to thank you all in advance for (5) s.. me.

                 Well, we've got a lot on the (6) a.. and I want to make as
                 much (7) p.. as possible in the next two hours or so.
                 If we stick to the main (8) s.., we should
                 (9) g.. everything and (10) a..
                 all of our (11) g.. and (12) o.. .
                 I will (13) c.. the meeting, as usual, but I really hope that you
                 will all have something to (14) c.. and if anything needs
                 (15) c.. please don't hesitate to
                 (16) i.. me (although not too often, I hope: the more
                 (17) i.. we can (18) a..
                 today the better).

                 I'll be (19) b.. several important
                 (20) m.. during the meeting, beginning with those that I
                 feel should take (21) p.., before
                 (22) s.. the main (23) p..
                 and making (24) r.. . This will be followed by an
                 (25) o.. session where you can give me your
                 (26) o.. . And I'm sure you will all be delighted to hear
                 that after the meeting (27) c.., there will be drinks and
                 snacks for everyone.

                 Mr Barker will be taking (28) n.. and keeping the
                 (29) m.. of the meeting, and I will be using these to write
                 my (30) r.. afterwards, so if anyone has any
                 (31) c.., I suggest you talk to him and not to me!

                 Now, before I start, are there any (32) q.. from the
                 (33) f.. ?

Participants: Zzz.

Money matters 1

Exercise 1

Exercise 1

Explain the differences between the words and phrases in **bold** in the following groups.

1. To **lend** and to **borrow**
2. **Inflation** and **deflation**
3. A **discount** and a **refund**
4. **Income** and **expenditure**
5. To be **insolvent** and to be **bankrupt**
6. A bank **statement** and a bank **balance**
7. To be **in the red** and to be **in the black**
8. An **invoice** and a **receipt**
9. To make a **profit** and to make a **loss**
10. **Gross** profit and **net** profit
11. To be **undercharged** and to be **overcharged**
12. Something which is **overpriced** and something which is **exorbitant**
13. To **save** money and to **invest** money
14. A **wage** and a **salary**
15. **Extravagant** and **economical**
16. A **loan** and a **mortgage**
17. A **loan** and an **overdraft**
18. **Shares** and **stocks**
19. **Commission** and **interest**
20. Something which is **worthless** and something which is **priceless**
21. To **credit** and to **debit**
22. A **pension** and **redundancy pay**
23. A **dividend** and a **royalty**
24. **Tax** and **duty**
25. To **deposit** money and to **withdraw** money
26. A **bill** and a **check**

Exercise 2

Complete these paragraphs with appropriate words or phrases from Exercise 1. In some cases you will need to change the form of the word, and in some cases more than one answer may be possible.

1. The store is happy to exchange faulty goods, but it can only offer customers a .... on production of a valid ....

2. *Customer:* Excuse me, miss. I think you've .... me.
    This .... says that my pizza cost $30.50.
    Waitress: That's correct sir. It's $25, plus a service charge of 10%, and government .... of 12%.
    Customer: Well I think that's an .... price to pay for a pizza!

3. This month's bank .... shows that we have an .... of $800. We can't afford to be ....
    to such a large amount. It's time we reduced our ....

4. Our sales representatives receive a basic .... (pre-tax)
    annual .... of $20,000, plus a 10% ....
    for each item they sell. On average, their ....
    (post-tax) .... is around $45,000 a year.

5. The company was declared .... after it was unable to pay off all its
    debts. Many people who lost their jobs as a result did not receive ....,
    and those who were about to retire lost half of their ....
    People who had .... heavily in the company saw
    their .... become completely ....

Also see *Money matters 2* on pages 33 and 34, *Earnings, rewards and benefits* on pages 16 and 17, and *Shopping and consumerism* on pages 48 and 49.

Money matters 2

Complete the sentences with words from the box. Write your answers in the crossword grid on the next page. To make this a bit more challenging, there are no black spaces in the crossword grid: just write the words following the directions of the arrows (⇨ or ⇩)

afford   assets   audit   bargains   budget   capital   charge   check
compensation   cost   credit   currency   debts   deducted
down payment   earnings   finances   fortune   funding   owes   profitable
rate   rebate   sponsored   subsidized   welfare   yield

1⇨   We have increased our publicity .... by $600,000, giving us a total of over $3 million to spend on advertising.

1⇩   The sale begins next week. Customers can expect some fantastic ...., including a home cinema package for less than $500.

2⇨   I didn't think the project would make us much money, but in fact it was extremely ...., and we made over $30,000!

3⇨   Before you start your own company, it is essential to have enough .... to start it up and keep it running until it begins to make a profit.

4⇩   The airline will offer passengers up to $500 .... for lost luggage or damage to personal property.

5⇨   The computer costs $1,500, but you do not need to pay for it all at once: you can make a .... of $200, and pay for the rest later.

6⇨   My job doesn't pay very well. In fact, my .... are barely enough to pay the rent.

7⇩   The latest art exhibition to be shown at the Metropolitan is a collection of photographs and paintings of chocolate. Not surprisingly, it is being .... by the country's biggest chocolate manufacturer, Hoggychocs.

8⇩   The .... of living goes up every year. This is partly due to inflation, and partly due to increased taxation.

9⇨   The company has lost a lot of money recently, and may be forced to sell some of its ...., including the company jet and two office blocks in Manhattan.

10⇨   The company .... the bank almost $2 million, which it is currently unable to pay back.

11⇨   Last year we paid too much tax (over $10,000 too much in total), so this year we hope to get a .... for the same amount.

12⇩   Payment can be made by cash, ... or credit card.

13⇩   The city has an excellent public transport system which is .... by local government so that it can keep its fares low.

14⇨   The company's .... are handled by an accountant from the one of the city's biggest financial firms.

14⇩   Many people think that all writers make a .... from their books, but unfortunately this is rarely true.

15⇩   The US dollar is very weak at the moment, so fewer people can .... to take a vacation overseas.

16⇨   Aviva Ltd is happy to offer new customers interest-free .... for the first six months. After that, an interest rate of 18% will apply.

17⇩   Every year the company's accounts are checked carefully for any mistakes. This annual .... also helps us to identify areas where we could improve our sales record.

18⇩   The city hopes to start building a new library next year, provided it can get government .... to begin the project. The minimum amount it hopes to receive is $750,000.

19⇨ Most people who lose their jobs end up on ...., although many say they are too embarrassed to receive government handouts.

20⇨ We have invested over $2 million in the company, but unfortunately the .... has been very low and we are considering selling our stocks.

21⇨ Thank you for your order. Your goods have been despatched, and the sum of $17.50 will be .... from your account within the next five days.

21⇩ Our .... are rapidly increasing. Last month they were $20,000, and this month they are $32,000. I don't know how we're going to pay them off.

22⇩ If you make a reservation in advance, the hotel can offer you a special .... of $85 a night, including breakfast.

23⇨ If your order costs over $50, delivery is free of ....

24⇨ When the dollar is strong it can buy more foreign ...., which means that more people are inclined to travel abroad.

Also see *Money matters 1* on page 32, *Earnings, rewards and benefits* on pages 16 and 17, and *Shopping and consumerism* on pages 48 and 49.

Obligation and option

Complete the sentences with a suitable word from the box. More than one answer is possible in some cases.

allowed	alternative	compelled	compulsory	entail	essential	exempt
forced	have	liable	mandatory	must	need	obligation	obliged
	optional	required	voluntary			

1.   A valid passport and visa are .... by all visitors to the country. Unless you have these, you will not be allowed in.

2.   The wearing of helmets and safety clothing on site is .... You may not enter the site without these.

3.   Note to hire car drivers: all passengers .... wear seatbelts. This includes rear-seat passengers. Your insurance will be invalid if you fail to comply.

4.   There are no direct flights between London and New Orleans. Passengers flying between these cities .... to change in New York or Washington.

5.   All companies are .... for the health and safety of their employees while on company premises, and can face heavy financial penalties if they fail to comply.

6.   Because of the recession, several companies in the area have been .... to close.

7.   Books, clothes and food are currently .... from government tax, as they are considered necessities rather than luxuries.

8.   .... safety inspections are carried out twice a year. Companies should allow government safety inspectors complete access to all areas.

9.   Entrance to the museum is free, but visitors are asked to make a .... donation of $10.

10. There is no service charge in this restaurant, but we do ask that groups of eight or more pay an ..:... 10% extra.

11. Unless you make prompt repayments, we will have no .... but to reclaim the property from you.

12. Manufacturers of packaged foods are .... to list all the ingredients clearly on the box or packet. This should include any artificial colorings and additives.

13. You are under no .... to work overtime, but we hope that you would be prepared to work late at least once a week.

14. When Mr Smith made a mistake that lost his company over $100,000, he felt .... to leave and look for work elsewhere.

15. The project is very exciting, but everyone realizes that it will .... a lot of work.

16. You can order our latest software programs by phone or on line. And the great thing is, there's no .... to pay until you've received your purchases.

17. It is absolutely .... that deliveries are made on time, otherwise we will start to lose customers.

18. Nobody is .... to talk in the studio while the red "recording" light is on.

Opposites 1: verbs and adjectives

Complete the sentences below with an <u>opposite</u> of the verb or adjective in **bold**, then write the words in the appropriate space in the tables. If you do this correctly, you will reveal two more words in the shaded vertical strips that are opposites of each other. (Note that in some cases, more than one answer may be possible, but only one will fit into each space in the table.)

1. A project can **fail** or it can ....
2. An object can be **solid** or it can be ....
3. A job can be **temporary** or it can be ....
4. A metal edge (on a knife, for example) can be **blunt** or it can be ....
5. You can **reward** somebody for good behavior, or you can .... them for bad behavior.
6. There are some things you can say in **private** that you should never say in ....
7. A surface can be **rough** or it can be ....
8. Calculations can be **exact** or they can be ....
9. You can **lend** something to somebody, or you can .... it from somebody.
10. In a court of law, a person can be found **innocent** or they can be found ....
11. A society can be **primitive**, or it can be ....
12. In an accident, you might suffer from a **major** injury or a .... one.
13. A pool of water can be **deep** or it can be ....
14. **Professional** sports people can make a lot of money, but .... ones do it for fun or pleasure.
15. Some students in the class were **absent**, but most of them were ....
16. Some foods contain **natural** flavorings, but many contain .... ones.
17. You can either .... or **reject** an offer.
18. You can **create** something or you can .... it.
19. You can **admit** doing something wrong, or you can .... it.

Opposites 2: adjective prefixes

A lot of adjectives can be made into their opposite form by adding a *prefix* (*un-*, *in-*, *dis-*, *il-*, etc) to the beginning of the word.

Exercise 1
Decide which of the prefixes from the first box can be used to make opposites of the words in the second box.

dis-	il-	im-	in-	ir-	un-

.....acceptable   .....accurate   .....adequate   .....advantaged   .....agreeable

.....attractive   .....authorized   .....avoidable   .....believable   .....certain

.....comfortable   .....competent   .....complete   .....conscious   .....contented

.....convincing   .....correct   .....curable   .....even   .....fair   .....fashionable

.....honest   .....inclined   .....legal   .....limited   .....literate   .....logical

.....married   .....mature   .....moral   .....mortal   .....obedient   .....organized

.....patient   .....perfect   .....personal   .....possible   .....proper   .....pure

.....qualified   .....rational   .....regular   .....relevant   .....replaceable

.....resistible   .....resolute   .....responsible   .....satisfactory   .....satisfied

.....sufficient   .....welcome

Exercise 2
Without looking at your answers to Exercise 1, look at the following sentences and paragraphs. In each one there is one underlined word which has been given the wrong prefix. Decide which word is wrong and correct it.

1.   He is a very (A) <u>disagreeable</u> man and he makes visitors feel very (B) <u>unwelcome</u>, but the management think he's (C) <u>irreplaceable</u> and are (D) <u>uninclined</u> to fire him.

2.   Insider dealing is not only (A) <u>immoral</u> and (B) <u>inhonest</u>, but also (C) <u>illegal</u>: companies are legally bound to take the strongest possible action against such (D) <u>unacceptable</u> behavior by their employees.

3.   It is an (A) <u>unavoidable</u> fact, but in a competitive job market, those who are (B) <u>unqualified</u> or who have (C) <u>imsufficient</u> work experience will find themselves seriously (D) <u>disadvantaged</u>.

4.   She was described by her boss as being (A) <u>unresponsible</u>, (B) <u>incompetent</u> and (C) <u>immature</u>, which she considered extremely (D) <u>unfair</u>.

5.   In return for an increased investment, the company offered (A) <u>unlimited</u> returns for their investors. While many found such an offer (B) <u>irresistible</u>, some thought the promises were (C) <u>innconvincing</u> and were (D) <u>uncomfortable</u> about parting with so much money.

6.   He had clearly given his presentation (A) <u>disadequate</u> preparation, and many in the audience challenged the points he made, saying they were (B) <u>inaccurate</u> and (C) <u>illogical</u>. Despite this, he remained (D) <u>irresolute</u> in his views, although the only person he managed to convince was himself.

Opposites 3: verb prefixes

Some verbs can be made into their opposite form, or otherwise modified, by the addition of the prefixes *dis-*, *im-* *mis-* or *un-*.

Complete each of the sentences below with one of the prefixes above and the *most appropriate* verb from the box. In most cases, you will also need to change the end of the verb (by adding *-s*, *-ed*, *-ing*, etc, and in some cases by also removing a letter). Use your answers to complete the crossword on the next page.

agree	allow	approve	behave	calculate	connect	continue
cover	diagnose	fold	judge	like	load	lock	obey	place
please	prove	qualify	quote	represent	trust	understand	use

1.   As the full extent of the company's financial problems ...., the management decided to take drastic action.

2.   The press have once again .... the President: he said that women were "America's hope for the future", and not "America's hopeless future".

3.   Unfortunately, many of our employees .... the new uniform, claiming it is old-fashioned and uncomfortable.

4.   It is a sad fact of office life that when the manager is away some employees feel free to
....

5.   Some staff members have .... several directives regarding punctuality, and can expect to be disciplined.

6.   We regret that our trust in your company was sadly ...., and therefore we will not be dealing with you in the future.

7.   The salesman accidentally .... the discount due to us, so we hardly broke even on the deal.

8.   Deliveries need to be .... from the truck as soon as they arrive, and placed in the storeroom on the first floor.

9.   It is dangerous to remove paper jams in the photocopier without first ....
the copier from the power supply.

10.   At first, I thought our new manager was lazy and incompetent, but I'm glad to say that I completely .... him. He is, in fact, one of the hardest working and most competent people I've ever met.

11.   Overseas business deals sometimes fail when one party .... the other's intentions, usually as a result of linguistic or cultural differences.

12.   The management .... of employees making private calls from the office.

13.   The company claimed $20,000 for fire damage, but the claim was ....
because proper safety procedures had not been observed.

14.   If any employee .... the company computers (e.g., for accessing undesirable Web sites), they will be instantly dismissed.

15.   Despite recent rumors in the press, Kaput Computers is pleased to announce that it will *not* be
.... its popular line of budget laptops.

16.   The lack of progress has .... the management, and in view of this they plan to review working procedures.

17. Employers have every right to .... job applicants who are not able to provide adequate references or show proof of their qualifications.

18. A recent company investigation has .... several cases of unauthorized Internet use during office hours.

19. Getting nowhere in your job? Then .... the secrets to business success with our new book, "The Only Way is Up!".

20. The National Patients' Association is calling on Senators around the country to make doctors legally responsible for .... an illness.

21. The press deliberately tried to .... our company, suggesting that we buy our products from factories which use child labor. This is simply not true.

22. New government legislation has been criticized for offering compensation to people who have been .... from driving and who have lost their jobs as a result.

23. The huge increase in exports recently has .... the argument that the world has stopped buying American goods.

24. If any employee .... with the new working regulations, they should speak to their line manager.

Ownership, giving, lending and borrowing

Rearrange the letters in **bold** in these sentences to make nouns and verbs related to ownership, giving, lending and borrowing. Write these words in the grid. If you do this correctly, you will reveal a word in the shaded vertical strip that can be used to complete the sentence at the bottom of the page.

1. **rotpePyr** prices in the city center have doubled in the last five years. As a result, many companies are choosing to set up in the suburbs, where land and buildings cost up to 40% less.

2. Calling all **rdoldlsan**! Do you have houses and apartments that are still empty? Do you want to fill these with reliable, trustworthy city workers and get a decent price? Then call "Rooftops" agency today!

3. Our department has been **coaltelad** $5,000 to buy new furniture and computers.

4. Employees will be **vopdried** with a uniform, which they should wear at all times when dealing with members of the public.

5. When you buy real estate you will need to take out a **gmtoerag**, unless you have enough money to pay for it up front.

6. Entrance to the museum is free, but we ask visitors to make a small voluntary **atidnono** of two or three dollars to help pay for its upkeep.

7. Guests are reminded that the hotel is not responsible for the loss of or damage to their personal **isssssepono**, and are advised to keep any valuables in the hotel safe.

8. Our company doesn't actually own the building we operate from. It's owned by Bigbucks Holdings Ltd, and we're just the **netsnat**.

9. Before we could start trading, we had to get a $100,000 **onal** from the bank to pay for the license and begin our advertising campaign.

10. Food at the party was free, but everyone was asked to **tircutoneb** $5 to pay for the drinks.

11. The shop is owned by the city council, but it is **eseadl** to a British company who sell sports equipment.

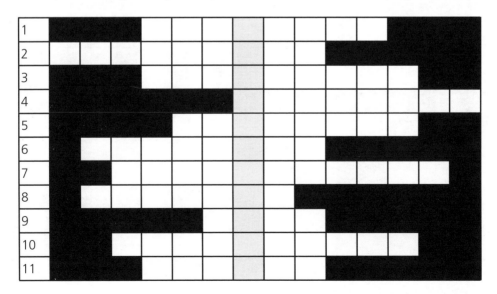

The word you should reveal in the shaded vertical strip can be used to complete this sentence:

.... of small, independent stores in towns and cities often complain that they are unable to compete with major stores and malls in the suburbs.

Phrasal verbs 1

Phrasal verbs are very common in English, and should be learnt like any other item of English vocabulary. They may appear at any stage in the TOEIC®. The exercises on the next three pages give you practice in some of the most common and useful phrasal verbs.

Complete the sentences below with a phrasal verb comprising *a verb* and *one or two particles* from the box. The meaning of the phrasal verb is explained in parentheses at the end of each sentence. In some cases, you will need to change the form of the verb (e.g., to past simple, present continuous, third-person 's', etc). In each sentence, the phrasal verb has one more letter than the previous sentence (i.e., the phrasal verb in number 1 has four letters, in number 2 it has five letters, in number 3 it has six letters, etc)

against	away	behind	call	come	cut	fall	fill	do	end
forward	get	go (x 2)	look	of	off (x 2)	out (x 2)		pull	run
	subject	through (x 3)		to (x 3)	up (x 3)		with (x 3)		

1. Prices are expected to .... by 20% next year. (*to rise / increase*)

2. Unless we reduce the amount of energy we use, we'll .... getting a huge bill at the end of the next quarter. (*to finish in a certain situation without wanting or intending to*)

3. We were in the middle of negotiations on the phone when we were suddenly .... (*to have a phone call stopped before it is finished*)

4. When you .... the application form, don't forget to include a daytime telephone number. (*to write information in the empty spaces on an official document*)

5. Unless we act soon, we'll .... options. (*to have nothing left*)

6. When the chairman realized half his staff would be absent from the meeting, he .... it .... (*to decide not to do something*)

7. If the country decides to .... customs inspections for goods from Canada, it may lead to the market being flooded with surplus goods. (*to get rid of something / remove something*)

8. The company was .... a lot of very difficult questions regarding its operating methods. (*to make somebody or something experience something unpleasant*)

9. We had to .... them the importance of keeping a proper filing system. (*to make someone understand – usually with difficulty – something important*)

10. A lot of companies complain that they often .... unnecessary bureaucracy and red tape when dealing with foreign companies. (*to have to deal with something difficult, often without expecting it*)

11. The economic recession almost destroyed a lot of smaller businesses, but thanks to government funding, many are now .... (*to recover*)

12. After looking carefully at the potential advantages and disadvantages of a merger, the directors eventually .... it. (*to do something you have planned to do*)

13. We are very much .... doing business with you. (*to be happy about something that will happen in the future*)

14. I've been out of the office for a few days, and now I'm .... my work. (*fail to make enough progress*)

Phrasal verbs 2

Complete the phrasal verbs in **bold** below with appropriate particles (in, out, up, etc). In each sentence, the particles you need are the same for each gap. Note that each of the phrasal verbs in number 10 needs two particles.

1.   We are **counting** .... you for your support, and we are also **relying** .... you to keep us informed of the latest developments, otherwise we are not sure we will be able to **go** .... working with you.

2.   At the meeting, the manager **pointed** .... that after he had **worked** .... the overall cost of the project, he had **figured** .... we would need to **pull** .... of the deal.

3.   While attempting to **set** .... its Miami department and **build** .... its customer base in the area, the company **ran** .... debts of almost $20 million.

4.   Global Travel Ltd cannot afford to **put** .... the issue of redundancy any longer: the international economic recession has **set** .... a series of problems, and the travel industry has **come** .... particularly badly.

5.   Before AVC Motors **took** .... the running of Varsie's Autos, it **went** .... its list of assets very carefully, but it failed to **look** .... the business premises.

6.   When management-union talks **broke** .... and the production lines had to be **shut** .... as a result, the people who had worked so hard to make the negotiations a success felt they had been badly **let** ....

7.   During the union dispute, the management said that they would rather **hand** .... their notice than **give** .... to union demands, but in the end they decided to **call** .... an independent arbitrator to deal with the unrest.

8.   If enough people **show** .... at tomorrow's meeting, I would like to **bring** .... the subject of pay increases: business has **picked** .... a lot recently, and I think it is only fair that our staff are rewarded.

9.   The company **ran** .... some unexpected financial difficulties, and when the accounts department **looked** .... the problem carefully, they discovered that a computer hacker had **broken** .... their files and stolen almost $2 million.

10. In order to **catch** .... our competitors and **keep** .... market developments, we will need to **put** .... increased production costs.

Now try using the phrasal verbs above in some of your own sentences. Make sure you use the phrasal verb in its correct form, paying particular attention to the tense of your sentence (for example, present continuous, past simple, present perfect, etc).

Don't forget to keep a written record of any new phrasal verbs you learn, and try to review and use them regularly so that they become an active part of your vocabulary.

Each of the following paragraphs uses four phrasal verbs in **bold**. However, one phrasal verb in each paragraph is incorrect because the wrong particle (*in*, *out*, *on*, etc) has been used. Identify and correct that particle in each case.

1. I **came across** the plans while I was **going up** some old files. I wanted to **throw them out**, but my boss told me to **hold on to** them in case they might be useful in the future.

2. The flight departure was **held up** because a group of tourists were late **checking into**, and by the time we eventually **took off**, it was **getting on for** almost 11 o'clock.

3. We need to **tighten up** security in the workplace, so over the next few months a series of new security measures will be gradually **phased in**. We're **bringing in** a firm which specializes in this field, and we're hoping it will **come up to** a workable program.

4. The company is **looking into** the possibility of opening a department in China to **deal with** the growing market for our products in the country. If we **go ahead** with this, we will then need to **build about** a reliable network of suppliers and carriers in the region.

5. We might have to **face up to** the fact that the deal with Automart might **fall up**. I've asked the committee to **check out** other options available to us if this happens, but we might have to **fall back on** our original plan.

6. The company is going to **bring apart** some of the best minds in the industry to **carry out** a survey looking at the possibility of expanding the company into Europe. They will then **put together** a series of measures and options available to us. Our main concern at the moment is how to **get round** the inevitable bureaucracy that will be involved.

7. I expect there will be a few problems, but these can probably be **smoothed out** without much difficulty. I must **put across** to everyone my view that we have no intention of **dropping in of** the project at this stage, and I suggest we **go about** this exciting challenge with enthusiasm and determination.

8. Because of economic difficulties, the company has **come under** severe financial pressure. This means that we need to **cut back** on staff in several departments, and so over the next two years, several positions will be gradually **phased out**. The unfortunate task of informing those who will have to leave **falls for** Ms Bailey, our Human Resources manager.

9. We hold regular staff training and development sessions after work which all employees have to **take part in**. Nobody can **opt out of** these unless they have work commitments. And the management becomes very suspicious if employees try to **get out of** any of the sessions by suddenly **coming through with** mystery "illnesses"!

10. Although he **came in** a lot of money when his father died, he decided to **carry on** working for the company. He enjoyed his work so much that he **turned down** the offer of promotion. However, he decided to leave when he **fell out** with his boss over plans to make several of his colleagues redundant.

11. The staff all **look up to** the company director: he's efficient, he's approachable and he's friendly. He **looks after** them like they were his own children, and is always happy to **sort out** any problems that they might have. In that respect, he **takes to** his father, who started the company in 1987.

12. When she didn't **turn round** for work for the third day in a row, we decided to **find out** what the problem was. It **turned out** that she was unhappy in her job because she felt the boss was always **picking on** her and making her life difficult.

Prepositions 1

Complete these sentences with the correct preposition.

1.   The next monthly meeting is .... 2 April.
      (A) **on**   (B) **at**   (C) **in**   (D) **with**

2.   Your completed application form must arrive .... 2 October at the latest.
      (A) **in**   (B) **at**   (C) **during**   (D) **by**

3.   The company has been running its Houston office .... the beginning
      of 2003.
      (A) **for**   (B) **at**   (C) **since**   (D) **in**

4.   Mrs Lebrowski is my boss: I've worked .... her for five years.
      (A) **over**   (B) **between**   (C) **through**   (D) **under**

5.   Traveling .... Europe by train is a wonderful and unique experience.
      (A) **by**   (B) **across**   (C) **at**   (D) **on**

6.   The hotel is happy to provide its guests .... complimentary soap,
      shampoo and other toiletries.
      (A) **with**   (B) **for**   (C) **under**   (D) **during**

7.   The average commuter journey .... work takes 47 minutes.
      (A) **by**   (B) **to**   (C) **at**   (D) **on**

8.   The duty manager is responsible .... dealing with any problems that
      customers have.
      (A) **about**   (B) **with**   (C) **against**   (D) **for**

9.   All office paperwork has to be filed: don't throw anything ....
      (A) **down**   (B) **out**   (C) **up**   (D) **over**

10.   The night train .... Washington DC arrives in Miami early the next morning.
      (A) **by**   (B) **with**   (C) **at**   (D) **from**

11.   Commuters rely .... a punctual, comfortable and safe public
      transport service to get them to work.
      (A) **on**   (B) **for**   (C) **about**   (D) **to**

12.   The seminar has been moved from Wednesday .... Friday.
      (A) **until**   (B) **for**   (C) **to**   (D) **by**

13.   Employees who are repeatedly absent .... work for no reason will
      have their wages reduced.
      (A) **about**   (B) **with**   (C) **at**   (D) **from**

14.   I always have a big evening meal, but for some reason I always wake up hungry
      .... the middle of the night.
      (A) **at**   (B) **on**   (C) **in**   (D) **to**

15.   The quickest way to get from New York to Chicago is .... air.
      (A) **by**   (B) **on**   (C) **in**   (D) **through**

16.   Your pay claim has to be approved .... the financial comptroller
      before she can give you any money.
      (A) **at**   (B) **for**   (C) **to**   (D) **by**

17.   The shopping mall has been running a very popular car valet service ....
      two months.
      (A) **before**   (B) **for**   (C) **since**   (D) **in**

18.   I was so tired that I slept .... most of the movie.
      (A) **through**   (B) **in**   (C) **between**   (D) **to**

19.   The manager is on a training course in Denver and will be back .... a few days.
      (A) **in**   (B) **at**   (C) **since**   (D) **until**

20.   Most Americans would rather stay home and watch TV .... the evening than go out.
      (A) **on**   (B) **in**   (C) **at**   (D) **to**

Prepositions 2

The sentences below each contain four underlined prepositions. One of the prepositions is not correct. *Identify* and *correct* that preposition in each sentence.

1.   Your new job will require you to travel all (A) <u>over</u> the world (B) <u>with</u> business, and you will have to work (C) <u>with</u> some difficult people (D) <u>in</u> some very boring places.

2.   The seminar, which will be held (A) <u>from</u> 9 o'clock and midday (B) <u>in</u> the Lincoln Conference Hall, will be presented (C) <u>by</u> Adam Klaus, an expert (D) <u>on</u> recent IT trends.

3.   Following a series of advertisements (A) <u>in</u> the local paper, over 100 people applied (B) <u>on</u> the position of exports coordinator, and the manager set himself the task of personally replying (C) <u>to</u> every one (D) <u>by</u> the end of the week.

4.   We're meeting (A) <u>with</u> a very important client (B) <u>in</u> half an hour, so I'm afraid I'm (C) <u>over</u> a lot of pressure (D) <u>at</u> the moment.

5.   The office is open Monday (A) <u>through</u> Friday (B) <u>from</u> 8.30 am (C) <u>to</u> 5.30 pm, but it is closed (D) <u>at</u> Wednesday afternoons.

6.   The report is due (A) <u>on</u> Monday morning, but it doesn't have to be presented (B) <u>to</u> the board of directors (C) <u>by</u> Wednesday afternoon, when they arrive (D) <u>for</u> the annual general meeting.

7.   The flight doesn't arrive (A) <u>in</u> Los Angeles (B) <u>until</u> midnight, so once passengers have collected their luggage (C) <u>from</u> the luggage reclaim and gone (D) <u>up</u> customs and immigration, public transport will have stopped running for the night.

8.   He complimented me (A) <u>on</u> my hard work, thanked me (B) <u>for</u> the help I had given him, wrote his email address (C) <u>at</u> the back of one of my business cards and asked me (D) <u>to</u> contact him when I got home.

9.   Most workers go (A) <u>with</u> bus or subway (B) <u>from</u> the suburbs (C) <u>to</u> the city center, but sometimes it is quicker to go (D) <u>on</u> foot.

10.   The chairman sat (A) <u>between</u> the manager and the union leader and did his best to answer questions (B) <u>from</u> the workers, although there were several angry employees (C) <u>among</u> them who did their best to prevent him (D) <u>for</u> speaking.

11.   The airline apologized (A) <u>for</u> the extended delay, told the passengers they were grateful (B) <u>about</u> their patience, and offered (C) <u>to</u> return part of their fare or give them a discount (D) <u>on</u> their next flight.

12.   The city is famous (A) <u>for</u> its beautiful architecture, is rich (B) <u>in</u> history and culture, and has a population which is justifiably proud (C) <u>for</u> its heritage and which always offers a warm welcome (D) <u>to</u> visitors.

13.   If guests are not satisfied (A) <u>with</u> the service they receive at any time (B) <u>during</u> their stay, they should speak (C) <u>to</u> a customer advisor, or alternatively discuss their problems (D) <u>at</u> the duty manager.

14.   International travelers often suffer (A) <u>from</u> minor stomach upsets when they are (B) <u>on</u> vacation, but this is usually the result of a sudden change (C) <u>for</u> their diet rather than poor standards of hygiene (D) <u>in</u> the kitchen.

Note that in the error recognition section of the TOEIC®, you are required to *recognize* the error in each sentence, but unlike the exercise above, you do <u>not</u> have to *correct* it.

Sales and marketing

Exercise 1
In the following sentences, the owner of a cell phone company is telling people about his company's latest model of phone. However, each sentence contains a spelling mistake. Identify and correct the word in each case. The first one has been done for you.

1. Everybody says that the market for cell phones is very cowded, and there is no more room or demand for new products. _cowded_ = _crowded_

2. However, we believe we've found a nich in the market for something a little bit different: a cell phone that lets you *smell* the person you're talking to! Wow!
    .... = ...

3. We call it the "Smell-O-Phone®", and you can find it in our latest brocure, along with some of our other models. .... = ...

4. It's the ultimate must-have opmarket accessory.
    .... = ...

5. We made the decision to start making it after extensive reserch into what people wanted from a cell phone in the 21st century. .... = ...

6. Of course, we won't sell many without a great deal of advertiseing.
    .... = ...

7. As a result, we're launching a major campain to let the public know all about it.
    .... = ...

8. We're going to premote the *Smell-O-Phone®* in any way we can.
    .... = ...

9. There are going to be comercials on all of the main radio stations and television channels.
    .... = ...

10. And advertisements in all the daily newspapers and major magazines.
    .... = ...

11. You won't be able to walk down the street without seeing one of our giant billyboards.
    .... = ...

12. And you won't even be able to visit the Internet without our plop-ups coming up on your screen all the time! .... = ...

13. We're also going to send mailshoots to everyone who has ever bought one of our phones in the past. .... = ...

14. And naturally we'll be making some sponsership deals with some of the country's major sporting teams. .... = ...

15. If we're lucky, we might even get a famous rock star, actor or sports personality to endoarse it for us. .... = ...

16. There will also be big posters at every pont of sale (including department stores and music stores).
    .... = ...

17. In fact, there probably won't be a single major retale outlet anywhere in the country that doesn't sell the Smell-O-Phone®! .... = ...

18. Our expert salesmen will be there to give potential customers their pich and persuade them that the Smell-O-Phone® is just what they need.
    .... = ...

19. There will be lots of special offers, including disconts on phone and talk-time packages.
    .... = ...

20. There will also be lots of giveways: free hands-free kits, free phone covers, free ring tones, and so on.
    .... = ...

21. Sales won't just be limited to the dommestic market.
    .... = ...

22. We expect to expot the *Smell-O-Phone*® to Europe, South America and, well, everywhere!
.... = ...

23. In fact, our overseas raps are already packing their suitcases and booking their flight tickets.
.... = ...

24. Eventually we hope to have the *Smell-O-Phone*® made under franshise in Europe, the Far East and South America. .... = ...

25. You might also like to know that in addition to the phone itself, there will be a whole range of *Smell-O-Phone*® merchantising, including *Smell-O-Phone*® t-shirts, *Smell-O-Phone*® trainers and even *Smell-O-Phone*® candy! .... = ...

26. They will all carry the famous *Smell-O-Phone*® brant.
.... = ...

27. And come in unique *Smell-O-Phone*® pakaging.
.... = ...

28. Check out our latest cattalog to see the whole range!
.... = ...

29. We think it's the best invention since the microchip, although obviously some people will tell you that it's just hipe, and we're making a lot of fuss about nothing.
.... = ...

30. They'll say that the *Smell-O-Phone*® is nothing more than a fat, and that this time next year nobody will want one! .... = ...

31. However, I just know it will sell well, and I bet our competiton is getting really worried.
.... = ...

32. Perhaps I can canvince you to buy one? Go on! You know it's just what you've always wanted!
.... = ...

33. Hmm, I can see you're somebody who is going to need a lot of perswading
.... = ...

Exercise 2

Match these dictionary definitions with some of the key words in Exercise 1. These key words will be the ones that you corrected.

1. A detailed list of products or services, often with pictures, prices, etc. ....
2. To say publicly that you support something or approve of it. ....
3. The box or packet that a product is sold in. ....
4. The place where a product or service is sold directly to the public. ....
5. The things that somebody says to encourage you to buy something. ....
6. Something that is very popular for a short time. ....
7. An excessive claim in advertising. ....
8. The people or companies who sell a similar product or service as you, and who want to do better than you. ....
9. The name of a well-known product (for example, Nike, McDonald's, etc).
....
10. A reduction in price on a product or service. ....
11. Giving money to a group or organization in exchange for the right to advertise at events, on clothes, etc. ....
12. Information that a company sends by post to lots of people who might want to buy their product or service. ....

Also see *Shopping and consumerism* on pages 48 and 49

Shopping and consumerism

Complete these sentence pairs with the most appropriate word or phrase in **bold**. In several cases you will need to change the form of the word (for example, by making it plural or changing the tense).

1. **chain / concession**
   (A) We don't have our own stores, but we operate .... in several major department stores across the state.
   (B) J. C. Hogget's is the most successful .... store in the state, with almost 30 outlets in 12 cities.

2. **consumer / customer**
   (A) The store is very popular and is always full of ....
   (B) Electronic .... goods such as stereo systems, televisions, computers and cameras can be bought very cheaply on the Internet.

3. **cost / charge**
   (A) Despite a fall in crude oil prices, some gas stations are still .... drivers too much for their gas.
   (B) Many people are surprised to learn that it doesn't .... a lot to set up your own Web site.

4. **spend / pay**
   (A) A lot of people .... too much money on fast food when there are far healthier options available in the stores.
   (B) The company .... a lot for its new computers, but believes it has been worth the investment.

5. **credit / debit**
   (A) The store is happy to offer regular customers instant .... at an attractive APR of only 13.5%.
   (B) Thank you for buying your camera from EasyCameras.com. The sum of $220 will be .... from your account within five working days.

6. **offer / discount**
   (A) Prices in most shops are fixed, but it is often possible to ask for a / an ....
   (B) Would you like a brand-new laptop for only $300? If you want to take advantage of this amazing .... then hurry to PC Perfect now!

7. **exchange / change**
   (A) Please check your .... carefully before leaving the store, as mistakes cannot be rectified later.
   (B) Jade Furnishings Ltd will only .... damaged goods if they were damaged before they left the store.

8. **price / cost**
   (A) It is usually cheaper to buy electronic goods on the Internet, where .... are generally lower than in the stores.
   (B) A lot of stores have been forced out of business because their .... (including rent, electricity and staffing) were too high.

9. **retail / wholesale**
   (A) The disks usually cost 50 cents each in the shops, but we buy them .... direct from the manufacturers for 20 cents each.
   (B) If you go to the store, the .... price is $250, but it can be up to 40% cheaper if you buy on line.

10. **for sale / on sale**
    (A) The building is .... for $600,000.
    (B) For all your office equipment needs, come to Berkshire and Hunt, where you will find a large range of products ....

11. **receipt / bill**
(A) When you pay, make sure that the store gives you a ....: you will need this if you have to return goods at a later date.
(B) Customers are reminded that all .... must be paid within 21 days.

12. **check / bill**
(A) That meal was delicious! Shall we ask the waiter for the .... now?
(B) Can I pay you with a $50 ....? I'm sorry I don't have anything smaller.

13. **charge / check**
(A) You can pay by cash or ....
(B) The advantage of paying with a .... card is that you don't have to pay for your goods immediately.

14. **economic / economical**
(A) Buying something in large quantities direct from the manufacturer is much more .... than buying from a store.
(B) Because of the ongoing .... situation, we regret that we will cease trading on 15 March.

15. **supply / stock**
(A) The item you have requested is currently out of ...., and we do not expect any further deliveries for two weeks.
(B) Hanratty's Food Stores is a major chain which .... the catering industry with the finest and freshest meat, fruit and vegetables.

16. **serve / service**
(A) The manager was unhappy when he learnt that some of his customers had to wait 15 minutes to be ....
(B) Fordley and Mantle are very proud of the quality of .... they offer their customers.

17. **demand / supply**
(A) Prices often go up when .... for a product rises.
(B) Prices often come down when .... of a product increases.

18. **purchase / merchandise**
(A) The store has a large range of designer .... available to the public at very low prices.
(B) Although New York is a popular shopping destination, visitors tend to limit their .... to one or two major items.

19. **return / refund**
(A) We regret to announce that we can only .... 75% of the original price of your goods if you are unhappy with them.
(B) If you need to .... anything to us, please make sure it is well-wrapped and you have paid sufficient postage.

20. **team / staff**
(A) If you have a query, please ask a member of ....
(B) The store has done well because it has an excellent management ....

21. **make / do**
Nowadays, most people .... their shopping in large malls outside the city.
The company .... so much money that it was able to set up a chain of stores across the country.

Also see *Sales and marketing* on pages 46 and 47.

Similar meanings 1: nouns

Being familiar with words and phrases which have a similar (or the same) meaning to each other will give you a big advantage in the TOEIC®, especially in the Reading Comprehension section. The exercises on the next few pages give you practice with some of the most common and useful examples of these.

<u>Exercise 1</u>

Look at sentences 1 – 15. These can either be completed with a word from box **A** *or* a word with a similar meaning from box **B**. Identify both the words that could be used. In some cases, you will need to add an *-s* to one or both of the words when you put them into the sentence.

A	B
accommodations agenda appointment assistance benefit customer discipline discount drop fault opposition proof proximity requirement work	advantage client closeness decline defect employment evidence help housing meeting order prerequisites resistance reduction schedule

1. We have a very busy .... / .... today, so I suggest we start as soon as possible.

2. The company provides free .... / .... for its staff.

3. We need to maintain .... / .... on the factory floor at all times, otherwise there is an increased risk of an accident occurring.

4. Thank you for your kind .... / .... I couldn't have done it without you.

5. There has been a sharp .... / .... in the number of people attending the staff development sessions.

6. The latest computer program has several .... / .... which need to be sorted out before it can be put onto the market.

7. There has been a lot of .... / .... to the new compulsory overtime plan.

8. There is no .... / .... to show that standards of living have improved.

9. Repeated orders are eligible for a 10% .... / .... on wholesale prices.

10. The hotel is popular with business people because of its .... / .... to the central business district.

11. I can't see you this afternoon because I have a / an .... / .... with the Board of Directors.

12. A lot of our .... / .... say that they are unhappy with the speed of our service.

13. When the company begins operations, it hopes to provide .... / .... for 300 people.

14. There are several .... / .... to working from home: you save on travel costs, for one thing.

15. If you want the job, a working knowledge of German is one of the main .... / ....

Exercise 2

Instructions as above.

A	B
acclaim choice code cooperation customer liability outlet overview priority problem question revision staff strategy term	change collaboration complication condition (short) description option patron personnel plan praise precedence query responsibility rules store

1. His latest film has received widespread
    .... / .... and is expected to become a
    major box office success.

2. The company .... / .... state(s) that
    no employee can leave his or her work station without asking for permission.

3. The hotel accepts no .... / .... for any
    damage to vehicles in the car park.

4. There are two .... / .... available to
    us: close the company or move to another location.

5. Our latest brochure provides a / an .... / ....
    of our latest products and a brief history of the company.

6. All .... / .... are requested to attend
    tomorrow's meeting, which will begin at two o'clock.

7. Thanks to our .... / .... with several
    affiliated companies, we have increased our turnover by 37%.

8. .... / .... are requested not to smoke
    in the restaurant.

9. We advise you to read the .... / .... of
    the contract carefully, and contact us if you disagree with any of the points covered.

10. If you have any .... / .... please ask a
    member of staff.

11. Selfwood's operates several .... / ....
    where you can buy a selection of our own goods along with a large range of branded varieties.

12. We had hoped that everything would run smoothly, but unfortunately there have been several
    .... / ....

13. Our .... / .... is to wait for prices to
    fall before putting the product onto the market.

14. Advertising is currently our main concern, and it should take
    .... / .... over everything else.

15. Is it necessary to make any .... / ....
    to the plan, or should we keep it as it is?

Exercise 3
Instructions as above.

A	B
achievement advertising assignment caliber category charisma disparity ending entitlement notion proceeds proficiency review specialist ultimatum	accomplishment (personal) appeal classification difference expert final demand earnings idea intellect and ability job publicity right skills termination write-up

1.   The restaurant has received several good .... / .... in the press, and is a firm favorite with visitors to the city.

2.   Our latest model is excellent, but without adequate .... / ...., we won't sell enough to cover production costs.

3.   We believe that the new manager's lack of .... / .... will have a negative effect on sales.

4.   The hotel has several room .... / ...., including five family rooms and two honeymoon suites.

5.   Poor long-term sales figures resulted in the .... / .... of the contract and the closure of two offices.

6.   If you leave the company, you will lose your .... / .... to a share of the profits.

7.   We would very much appreciate having somebody of your .... / .... working for us: you would be of great benefit to the company.

8.   We called in a health and safety .... / .... to examine the building for any potential problems.

9.   He was given the .... / .... of dealing with the press and keeping the public informed about new developments.

10.   The new manager has a strange .... / .... that all employees are potentially dishonest.

11.   She hasn't reached the required level of .... / .... in typing, and will have to repeat that section of the training course.

12.   His promotion to director was a remarkable .... / .... for someone so young.

13.   The bank gave us a / an .... / .... to pay back the money or face immediate closure.

14.   Despite several changes to the pay structure, there is still a .... / .... in pay between graduate trainees and non-graduates.

15.   All .... / .... from the sale of the building will be reinvested in the company.

When you keep a written record of words that you learn, you might find it useful to put them into related groups. This would include putting words with the same or a similar meaning together. Remember that you should also record words in context (you should show how they work in a sentence with other words).

Similar meanings 2: verbs

Look at the words and phrases in **bold**, then arrange the letters in *italics* to make words which have the same or a similar meaning <u>in the same context</u>. Use these words to complete the crossword on the next page.

Across (⇨)

1. **Examine** accounts. *iuatd*

2. **Account for** something that has happened. *inelaxp*

5. **Recover** lost money or property. *eaimrcl*

6. **Advertise** a product. *eportom*

9. **Help** a customer. *sasits*

11. **Use up** all your resources. *usehaxt*

15. **Firmly state** your opinion. *artses*

17. **Prevent** a strike from happening. *vetar*

18. **Firmly tell** somebody your terms and conditions. *taitedc*

19. **Acquire** or **get** information. *anibto*

21. **Have an effect on** someone or something. *eniceflun*

22. **Manage** or **organize** a department. *dmaisteinr*

24. **Produce** or **make** good sales of a product. *agrtenee*

25. **Choose** something. *etslce*

27. **Understand** or **achieve** something. *izaerel*

29. **Tell** somebody about an event that has happened. *atlree*

31. **Quantify** the effect of something. *urmaees*

34. **Forbid** smoking in a public place. *nab*

35. **Give** information or instructions to your staff. *ribfe*

36. **Confirm** something is true. *ifrvey*

38. **Widen** your area of operations. *asienecr*

40. **Ask** somebody for advice. *ucltons*

41. **Approve** of a decision. *denseor*

42. **Oblige** somebody to do something. *qreueri*

43. **Give** or **take** a message to somebody. *nvceyo*

44. **Remove** something from a sum of money. *ucddte*

Down (⇩)

1. **Speak** to an audience. *daesdrs*

2. **Take on** new staff. *moelyp*

3. **Give** a contract to a company. *ardaw*

4. **Interrupt** somebody at work. *irbstdu*

7. **Check** facts to see if they are true. *ceainrast*

8. **Collect** information. *eagtrh*

10. **Replace** something with something similar. *tutsuetibs*

12. **Make** a process **go faster**. *ratccaeele*

13. **Deal with** a problem. *headln*

14. **Control** a process or activity. *egrutela*

16. **Come to** an interview. *tntaed*

20. **Make up for** something you have done wrong. *pecotensma*

23. **Book** a restaurant table. *rvreese*

26. **Keep** something for future use. *tarnei*

28. **Suggest** something without saying it directly. *yilmp*

29. **Disclose** information to somebody. *earelv*

30. **Make** something **clearer**. *afclyri*

32. **Examine** information in detail. *nzealay*

33. **Settle** an argument or disagreement. *srveoel*

37. **Finish** making plans for something. *liznfaie*

39. **Agree** to do something. *enosnct*

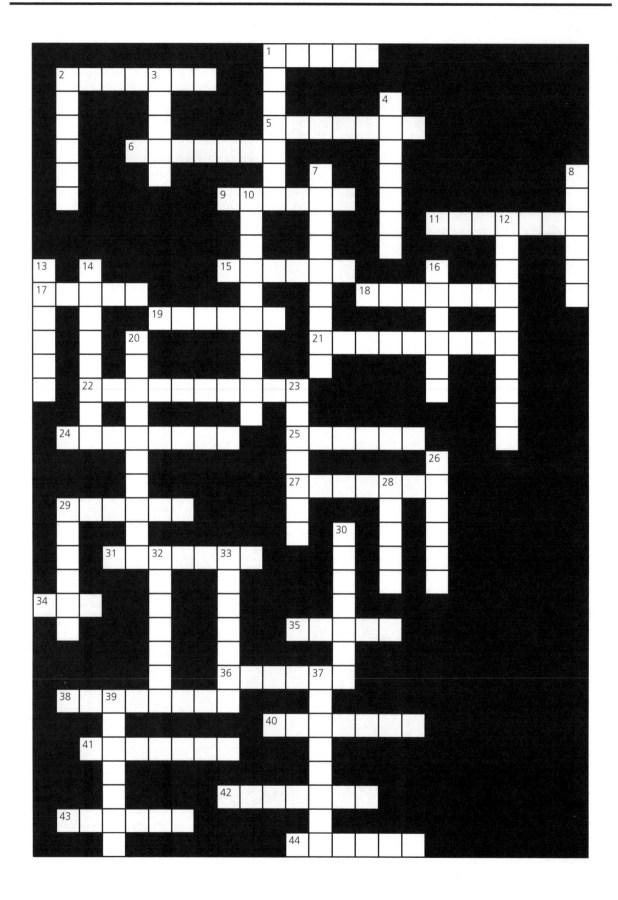

Similar meanings 3: adjectives

Exercise 1
Match the words or phrases in **bold** in 1 – 24 with words from the box which have a similar meaning. You should use each word from the box *once only*.

compatible	disciplinary	disparate	diverse	efficient	exceptional
flexible	important	industrious	integral	inventive	legitimate	lengthy
mandatory	modern	nominal	obligatory	perceptive	profitable
prosperous	punctual	steady	tedious	voluntary	

1. **Compulsory** safety inspections.
2. A **very important** part of something.
3. A **well-run and productive** department.
4. Two **well-suited** organizations.
5. **Compulsory** attendance at a meeting.
6. A **long** meeting.
7. A **creative** idea.
8. A **significant** event.
9. A collection of **unrelated** objects.
10. A **wealthy** town.
11. A **valid** reason for doing something.
12. An **optional** dress code.
13. A **constant and continuous** price rise.
14. An **outstanding** performance.
15. A **varied** program of events.
16. **Easily changeable** working hours.
17. A **lucrative** venture.
18. **Punitive** action.
19. A **boring and repetitive** job.
20. A **prompt** start to a meeting.
21. A **small** membership fee.
22. An **observant** young man.
23. A course of **contemporary** world studies.
24. A **hardworking** staff member.

Exercise 2
Instructions as above.

abrupt	abundant	adequate	crucial	discourteous	enduring
extensive	inconsistent	inflexible	luxurious	narrow	outdated
overall	prospective	relevant	resolute	restricted	risky	rudimentary
scrupulous	simple	thorough	thriving	vibrant	

1. A **lively** office atmosphere.
2. A **basic** menu.
3. A **determined** effort.
4. **Very comfortable** accommodations.
5. A **likely or possible** job applicant.
6. **Limited and controlled** access to a building.
7. A **flourishing** tourist industry.
8. A product's **lasting** appeal.
9. A **comprehensive** search.
10. **Basic** knowledge.
11. A **pertinent** question.
12. **Enough** information.
13. A **sudden** change of plan.
14. **Old-fashioned** working practices.
15. The **general** idea.
16. A financially **dangerous** plan.
17. **Plenty of** opportunities.
18. A **small** profit margin.
19. **Erratic** behavior.
20. A **rigid** schedule.
21. A **very important** meeting.
22. A **full or very detailed** investigation.
23. An **impolite** shop assistant.
24. An **honest and fair** dealer.

Starting and stopping

Exercise 1

The box below contains 36 words and phrasal verbs related to *starting* or *stopping* something. Try to find as many as possible. You will find them by reading from left to right and from right to left, following the directions of the arrows. To help you, the words and phrases appear in alphabetical order.

Start ⇨	A	B	O	L	I	S	H	A	R	I	S	E	B	A	⇰
⇦ E	S	A	E	C	L	E	C	N	A	C	T	U	O	K	C	⇱
⇩ C	L	O	S	U	R	E	D	E	L	E	T	E	D	E	T	⇰
⇦ S	I	D	E	U	N	I	T	N	O	C	S	I	D	R	E	⇱
⇩ M	I	S	S	D	I	S	S	U	A	D	E	E	M	B	A	⇰
⇦ B	A	T	S	E	E	T	A	C	I	D	A	R	E	K	R	⇱
⇩ L	I	S	H	F	I	R	E	F	R	E	E	Z	E	I	N	⇰
⇦ K	E	T	A	I	T	I	N	I	N	O	I	T	P	E	C	⇱
⇩ I	C	K	O	F	F	L	A	U	N	C	H	O	U	T	B	⇰
⇦ E	S	A	H	P	N	I	E	S	A	H	P	K	A	E	R	⇱
⇩ O	U	T	P	U	L	L	O	U	T	Q	U	A	S	H	Q	⇰
⇦ S	E	R	I	T	E	R	N	G	I	S	E	R	T	I	U	⇱
⇩ E	T	O	F	F	S	E	T	U	P	S	U	P	P	R	E	⇰
⇦ F	F	O	E	K	A	T	D	N	E	P	S	U	S	S	S	⇱
⇩ T	A	K	E	U	P	T	E	R	M	I	N	A	T	E	T	⇰
					Stop	N	W	O	D	N	R	U	⇱

Exercise 2

Now use the words and phrases from Exercise 1 to complete these sentences. In many cases, more than one answer is possible. Note that in the case of the verbs, you will need to change the form of some of them (for example, by adding *-ed* to the end).

1. We .... the contract with our suppliers when they repeatedly failed to deliver on time.

2. I can't find the document anywhere on my computer. I must have accidentally .... it.

3. We had to cancel the project when the investors .... and refused to give us any more money.

4. Because of an .... of food poisoning recently, the staff cafeteria will be closed until further notice.

5. The company was .... in 2002.

6. Before .... on a long journey, it is very important to make sure you have everything you need.

7. Several of the airline's crews told the press that they were concerned about the safety of its aircraft, but the airline's owner managed to .... the story before it went public.

8. As a result of increased security and a bigger police presence, crime has been almost completely ....

9. The store installed security cameras to .... shoplifters, but without much success.

10. We tried to .... the manager from making changes to the company structure, but he said he had already .... the first stage of the plan.

11. Our latest cell phone will be .... onto the market next month, and we are confident that sales will rapidly ....

12. Following a series of minor workshop accidents, production was temporarily .... while the machinery was checked for faults.

13. I .... photography as a hobby when I was 13, and by the time I was 15, I had already decided to make it my career.

14. The new regulations will not all begin at once: they will be gradually .... over the next two years. Meanwhile, the old overtime system will be gradually ....

15. Between its .... in 1925 and its eventual .... in 2011, World Film Studios made over 300 movies.

16. The company .... trading in 2008 because of poor sales and consequent financial troubles.

17. Mr Vettriano is 64, so I guess he'll be .... soon. I think he'll miss working here, though.

18. *Secretary:* "That's it! I've had enough of this place. I .... !"
    Manager: "Oh really? Well, I'm not going to give you the chance. You're .... !"

19. They made an excellent offer, but we were obliged to .... it .... because we were working on too many other projects.

20. Prices have risen rapidly over the last year, but last week the company announced a price ....: they have promised no more increases until April next year.

21. Banana Computers no longer make the Banana 127V printer: it's been ....

22. When Congress decided to .... the old tax laws, smaller companies suddenly found themselves much better off.

23. We have a lot of things to discuss at this meeting, so I suggest we .... immediately with a report on last year's sales.

24. Several problems have .... recently as a result of moving our distribution warehouse: one of these is the slow despatch time for overseas orders.

Also see *Continuing, repeating and starting again* on pages 10 and 11.

Travel 1

Exercise 1

Read this extract from a magazine article about travel, and <u>underline</u> the correct words or phrases in **bold**. Some of the words / phrases are wrong, some have the wrong form, and some have been spelt incorrectly. Note that in some cases, more than one answer is possible.

More people are traveling (1) **abroad / aboard** in the 21st century than ever before. Going away on (2) **vacating / vacation** for one or two weeks has never been easier, and the age of (3) **mass / massive** tourism has truly arrived! If you prefer the comforts of home and have never been away before, here's how it works.

If you enjoy the convenience of a (4) **packing / package** tour (where you pay for your flights, (5) **transfers / transits** to and from the airport, and (6) **acommodation / accomodation / accommodation** in advance), you simply go to the travel (7) **operator / agency**, pick up a (8) **brochure / catalog** or two, find a (9) **destiny / destination** and (10) **itinerary / itinerant** that suits you, and (11) **reserve / book** it. You then (12) **pay a deposit / make a down payment**, and pay the (13) **remainder / balance** closer to your travel date. Just before you (14) **leave / depart**, your tickets arrive and then you're away.

If you are an (15) **independence / independent** traveler who prefers more freedom and (16) **flexibleness / flexibility**, log on to the Internet, find a Web site that sells cheap flights, choose your (17) **departure / departing** date and return date, then pay the (18) **airfee / airfare**. You will then automatically have an (19) **A-ticket / E-ticket** logged with the airline. If you choose a hotel at the same time, your chosen hotel will automatically be informed of your (20) **booking / reservation**. You should also receive (21) **consternation / confirmation** of everything by email. Closer to the date of your (22) **trip / excursion**, some airlines will even let you (23) **check in / check-in** on line, to save you from queuing for ages at the airport (24) **terminus / terminal**. (25) **Ticketless / Ticketfree** travel has eliminated the need for piles of unnecessary paperwork. It's all so easy!

Or is it? Here are just a few things that you ought to consider (and remember, this all has to be done before you even get to the airport!).

First of all, you will need to check your passport: have you got one, for a start, and is it still (26) **validated / valid**? Most countries will not let you in if your passport (27) **runs out / expires** within six months. Secondly, what about a (28) **visa / visor**? More and more countries require you to have one, and this will cost you money (and time and effort, too: in some cases, you have to present yourself in person at the country's (29) **emmbassy / embassy**). Thirdly, you will need to get (30) **traveler's checks / traveling checks** and / or foreign (31) **currancy / currency**: if you choose the latter, you need to check the (32) **exchange / changing** rate to make sure you are getting a favorable (33) **deal / bargain**, and then in most cases you will need to pay (34) **comission / commission / commision** to the bank who supplies it. Finally, have you got adequate (35) **insurence / insurance / insureance** cover, are your (36) **vaccinations / vaccinnations / vacinations** up to date, will your cellphone work abroad, and have you made (37) **arrangments / arangements / arrangements** for someone to look after your cat and dog, and water your plants, while you are away?

<u>Exercise 2</u>
Without looking back at Exercise 1, complete these definitions with words and phrases from that exercise.

1.   A traveler who makes his / her own travel arrangements without needing help or advice from a travel agency is known as an .... traveler.

2.   A ticket for a journey that is stored on a computer and not given to the passenger is called an ....

3.   The money you pay for a flight is called an ....

4.   .... is a word that means "in another country".

5.   When large numbers of tourists visit a popular destination, this is called .... tourism.

6.   .... is money that you pay a bank or exchange bureau for changing your currency into another currency.

7.   The rate at which one currency can be exchanged for another currency is called the .... rate.

8.   A .... is an injection or other form of medical treatment which protects you from dangerous or unpleasant illnesses and diseases.

9.   A .... is a building at an airport where planes arrive or depart.

10.   A .... vacation is a vacation where you pay for your flight, hotels, etc, in one go and before you leave.

11.   When you ...., you show you are ready to get on a flight by giving your ticket to someone at the airport.

12.   .... is an adjective which means that a document is legal and can be used.

13.   A .... or .... is an arrangement you make for a room in a hotel, a table in a restaurant, etc.

14.   A .... is a general word for a journey (usually for a short period of time).

15.   When somebody tells you that something is certain (for example, they tell you that you have definitely got a room in their hotel), we say that they send you ....

Also see *Travel 2* on page 60 and *Hotels* on pages 22 and 23.

Travel 2

Underline the most appropriate word or phrase in **bold** in these sentences. In some cases, more than one answer is possible.

1. (*At the airport. A check-in assistant is talking to a passenger*) I'm afraid your flight has been **canceled / delayed / crashed / bumped**. It won't be leaving for another two hours.

2. (*At the airport. An angry passenger is talking to her colleague*) I don't believe it. The airline has **diverted / overbooked / rerouted / postponed** our flight and I've been told there are no more seats available for us. We'll have to wait for the next one.

3. (*A business executive is explaining why he prefers to fly business class*) Flying business class is much more expensive than flying **tourist / coach / economy / club** class, but it's much more comfortable and the food is better.

4. (*An announcement is being made at a seaport*) The ship will soon be ready for **embarkation / disembarkation / boarding / climbing**. Would passengers please ensure they have their tickets ready and proceed to the gate.

5. (*At the airport, an announcement is being made to passengers arriving on a flight*) Welcome to Heathrow Airport. Could we remind **transition / transitive / transitory / transit** passengers to wait in the lounge until their next flight is ready.

6. (*At the airport, an assistant is helping a passenger to find the right terminal for her flight from New York to Boston*) Terminal 1 is the terminal for international flights. You need terminal 2 for **domesticated / domestic / domesticity / domicile** flights.

7. (*At the station, a clerk is explaining ticket prices to a passenger who wants to visit a town and return on the same day*) A one-way ticket to Harrington costs $27.50. A **triangle-trip / round-trip / circle-trip / square-trip** ticket will cost you $42.

8. (*At the bank, a clerk is telling a customer why he can't take out any more money with his charge card*) I'm really sorry, sir, but you have already exceeded your **profit margin / loyalty points / credit limit / commission rates**.

9. (*On an aircraft, the captain is talking to his passengers*) If you need anything during the flight, please do not hesitate to ask one of our cabin **staff / gang / team / crew** members.

10. (*A radio announcement is being made for people traveling to a city for their job*) Bad news for **expatriates / commuters / immigrants / migrants**, I'm afraid. Traffic on the freeway is locked solid for 12 miles.

11. (*An article in a magazine is talking about air travel*) In a recent survey, Albion International Air Ltd was voted the world's favorite **carrier / airline / airliner / airways**, achieving top marks for its punctuality, comfort, quality of in-flight catering and, of course, its standards of safety.

12. (*A travel agent is explaining insurance policies to a customer*) We advise you to take out our **comprehensive / adhesive / apprehensive / defensive** insurance policy which will cover you against anything, or almost anything, that is likely to happen.

13. (*A tour operator is announcing its new range of environment-friendly holidays*) **Eco-tourism / Environmental tourism / Responsible tourism / Green tourism** has become so popular recently that we have added this to our range of holidays.

14. (*A car hire clerk is helping a customer choose a vehicle*) The roads here are so bad and so full of holes that we very much recommend you hire a / an **MPV / sedan / SUV / station wagon**.

Also see *Travel 1* on pages 58 and 59.

Word forms 1: nouns from verbs

The verbs in the top box can all be made into nouns by removing and / or adding letters. Decide on the noun form of each verb, and then write it (in its noun form) in the appropriate section of the table, depending on the changes that are made to it. There are five words for each section of the table, and there are <u>ten words</u> that <u>do not fit</u> into any section of the table.

abolish	acquire	admire	apply	argue	arrive	assure	attend	behave
choose	coincide	compete	consult	consume	criticize	decide	determine
disturb	emphasize	expand	expect	expose	fail	identify	imply
intervene	justification	lose	maintain	manage	negotiate	notify	permit
persuade	prefer	produce	prohibit	promote	provide	qualify
recognize	recommend	refuse	rehearse	relax	require	respond
scrutinize	sign	solve	subscribe	suggest	supervise	survive	warn

Remove 2 letters, then add 4 letters:	(Example: conclu~~de~~ ➜ conclude ➜ conclusion) ....
Remove 1 letter, then add 7 letters:	(Example: verify ➜ verif~~y~~ ➜ verif<u>ication</u>) ....
Remove 1 letter, then add 5 letters:	(Example: examine ➜ examin~~e~~ ➜ examin<u>ation</u>) ....
Remove 1 letter, then add 4 letters:	(Example: reduce ➜ reduc~~e~~ ➜ reduc<u>tion</u>) ....
Remove 1 letter, then add 3 letters:	Example: concentrate ➜ concentrat~~e~~ ➜ concentrat<u>ion</u>) ....
Remove 1 letter, then add 2 letters:	(Example: disperse ➜ dispers~~e~~ ➜ dispers<u>al</u>) ....

Add 3 letters:	(Example: depart ➜ depar<u>ture</u>) ....
Add 4 letters:	Example: improve ➜ improve<u>ment</u>) ....
Add 5 letters:	(Example: confirm ➜ confirm<u>ation</u>) ....

The 10 words that do not fit into any section of the table above are:

....

....

Exercise 2

Now take the verbs that did *not* fit into any section of the table, change them into nouns and write them in the grid below (in the same order that they appear in the box). If you do this correctly, you will reveal a word in the **shaded** vertical strip that can be a verb and a noun *without changing its form*.

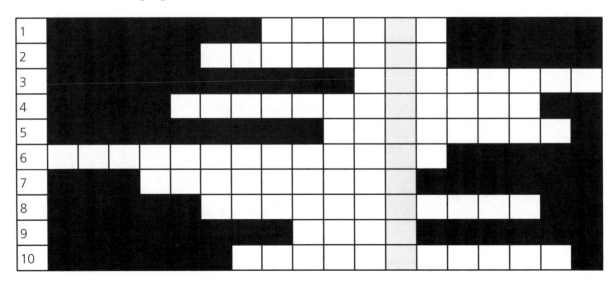

Now try using some of the words from this exercise in sentences of your own.

Word forms 2: nouns from adjectives

<u>Exercise 1</u>

Look at these sentences and decide if the words in **bold** are the correct *noun* form of the *adjectives* which you will find in parentheses at the end of each sentence. Correct those which are wrong. Look at the meaning of the whole sentence before you make any changes, and don't forget to check the spelling.

1.   Items of **valuability** can be left in the hotel safe overnight. (valuable) ....

2.   *La Poubelle d'Or* is the only restaurant in town for those with real **taste**! (tasteful)
        ....

3.   Do you have a **thirstiness** for knowledge? Then why not enroll on one of our evening college courses? (thirsty) ....

4.   It is often said that "**honestly** is the best policy", which is why AZ Enterprises have adopted it as its company motto. (honest) ....

5.   It can often be lack of **confidence** that prevents an employee performing well at work. (confident)
        ....

6.   Many people who start up their own company are unaware of the **expensiveness** involved. (expensive) ....

7.   Senior citizens can travel free on public transport between 9 am and 4 pm, although some **restrictions** apply. (restricted) ....

8.   There are a few **similarties** between our old TZ18b model and the new TZ20. (similar)
        ....

9.   The management are unable to say with any **certainess** when the new changes will be implemented. (certain) ....

10.   Unnecessary **absenteeism** from work is costing American companies millions of dollars a year. (absent) ....

11.   Please complete the form and return it at your earliest **convenientcy**. (convenient)
        ....

12.   The union has questioned the **necessaryness** of downsizing, but the management insists it is the only way to keep the company going. (necessary) ....

13.   Despite a **relaxation** of company rules regarding dress, many still prefer to wear a suit to work. (relaxed) ....

14.   Sometimes in business, rules have to be changed according to needs: **flexiblence** is the key to success. (flexible) ....

15.   Health and **safety** issues should be a priority with any organization. (safe)
        ....

16.   The management accepts no **responsibleness** for items lost or stolen in the workplace. (responsible) ....

17. In advertising, **accuracy** is very important when it comes to identifying the target market. (accurate) ....

18. The legal **profession** is often criticized for concentrating on making money instead of upholding the law. (professional) ....

19. There have been unforeseen **complicatenesses** with our new building proposal owing to opposition from environmental groups. (complicated) ....

20. Do you know the **differents** between *net* profit and *gross* profit? Is *overtime* the same as *allowed time*? If you answered "no" to the first and "yes" to the second, it's time you joined our "Business Basics" course! (different) ....

Exercise 2

Change the adjectives in the box into nouns following the instructions in the table. Each instruction relates to <u>3</u> of the adjectives in the box.

able aggressive appreciative available aware bored comfortable compatible confused considerate convenient creative deep familiar fashionable functional high hot logical long loyal mature optimistic optional pessimistic popular punctual realistic secure serious strong sufficient systematic true warm weak

Remove 4 letters:	
Remove 3 letters, then add 5 letters:	
Remove 3 letters, then add 1 letter:	
Remove 2 letters, then add 5 letters:	
Remove 2 letters, then add 3 letters:	
Remove 2 letters, then add 2 letters:	
Remove 2 letters:	
Remove 1 letter, then add 3 letters:	
Remove 1 letter, then add 2 letters:	
Add 2 letters:	
Add 3 letters:	
Add 4 letters:	

Try to use some of the words above in some of your own sentences.

Word forms 3: adjectives from verbs

Change the verbs in **bold** into their correct adjective form so that they are grammatically correct in the context of the sentences.

1. At the meeting we were shown a lot of **promote** .... material, but it wasn't very **inspire** ....

2. Recently, there have been some **innovate** .... and **impress** .... plans to change the working environment.

3. In the interests of the environment, our office staff need to change their **waste** .... habits, so we are introducing an **oblige** .... code for recycling and cutting down on waste.

4. The job was very **repeat** ...., and as a result it quickly became very **bore** ....

5. Everybody was very **excite** .... when we were offered the contract, but I was a little **doubt** .... it would go ahead.

6. Our new director isn't very **decide** ...., and needs to play a more **act** .... role in the day-to-day running of the company.

7. Computer software designers need to be far more **invent** .... if they want to keep up with a changing and **change** .... market.

8. The photocopier has stopped working five times this week, and the air-conditioning hasn't been working for a month: these **continue** .... copier breakdowns, coupled with the **continue** .... heat, have resulted in a lot of short tempers.

9. The financial comptroller isn't very **approach** .... In fact, some employees find him a little bit **frighten** ....!

10. Her argument wasn't very **convince** ...., and several of her colleagues were extremely **criticize** .... of her suggestions.

11. The market for all-**include** .... holidays (in which customers pay for their flight, accommodation, meals and drinks in advance) has become very **compete** ....

12. Our boss is very **help** .... and **support** ...., but unfortunately he isn't very **depend** ....

13. The mistake was easily **rectify** ...., but it would have been far more **prefer** .... if it hadn't happened in the first place.

14. Prices are non-**negotiate** ...., and you will need to pay a non-**refund** .... deposit of $500 before we can dispatch the goods.

15. There is **restrict** .... access to the building, and all visitors will need to show a **validate** .... pass and some form of ID.

16. Participation in the evening training seminars is entirely **volunteer** ...., but we hope that everyone will attend these highly **construct** .... sessions.

17. The accident was **avoid** ...., and it wouldn't have happened if you hadn't been so **care** ....

18. He's a very **create** .... and **imagine** .... manager, and his track record is **admire** ....

19. When you apply for a job, it is very important to be **specify** .... about your **occupy** .... qualifications and any previous experience.

20. The job is full-time, and offers an **attract** .... salary and other **excel** .... benefits, including a company car and free healthcare package.

Workplace problems

In the following sentences and paragraphs, one of the words in each of the word pairs in **bold** is *wrong* and one is *right*. <u>Underline</u> the most appropriate word in each case. You will find this easier to do if you read each paragraph through first so that you have a better idea of what it is about. (Note that the wrong words are real English words, but do not fit into the context of the sentence / paragraph.)

Paragraph (A)

If there is a (1) **despite / dispute** between the management and the union in a company which cannot be (2) **restored / resolved**, and as a result a (3) **strike / stroke** looks likely, a third party might be called in to (4) **abdicate / arbitrate**.

Paragraph (B)

Poor (1) **timekeeping / timeserving**, persistent (2) **abstentions / absenteeism** and general (3) **misconception / misconduct** at work have lost us over $200,000 this year.

Paragraph (C)

Three managers have been accused of (1) **fraught / fraud**, (2) **dissemination / discrimination**, (3) **bullying / bumbling**, (4) **racy / racial** (5) **obtuse / abuse** and (6) **sectional / sexual** (7) **harassment / arrestment**. As a result, two of them have been (8) **fried / fired** and one has been (9) **suspected / suspended** without pay. The first two are claiming (10) **unfair / unfaithful** (11) **dismissive / dismissal** and plan to (12) **appeal / appal**. The third has applied for a job with the government.

Paragraph (D)

We would like to point out that there have been several (1) **breaches / beaches** of the company's "no smoking" policy. We also have proof that several factory floor workers have been (2) **neglecting / negotiating** their duties, and there have also been several incidences of (3) **insurrection / insubordination** towards senior managers and intentional (4) **damning / damage** of company property. If this happens again, those responsible will be taken before a (5) **disconcerting / disciplinary** (6) **broad / board** and could face (7) **instant / instance** (8) **dismal / dismissal**.

Paragraph (E)

The management is fully aware that because of staff (1) **shortness / shortages** we are all (2) **overstretched / oversubscribed** at the moment, Mr Harrington, but we suggest that if you have a (3) **grievance / grievous**, you put it to us in writing rather than encourage your colleagues to hold a sudden (4) **walkout / walkabout**. We'd like you to treat this as a (5) **verbal / verdant** (6) **warming / warning**: the next time it happens, we will be obliged to ask for your (7) **notice / note**.

Paragraph (F)

What a terrible month! Sales have (1) **droned / dropped** by 40%, six employees have been made (2) **recumbent / redundant**, two senior managers have (3) **resigned / resided**, our main supplier has gone (4) **bankrolled / bankrupt**, someone has (5) **haggled / hacked** into the company Web site and given us a (6) **virus / viscous** (with the result that the entire computer system has (7) **crashed / cracked**), and the donut machine is still out of (8) **odor / order**.

Answers

Changes 1 (pages 1 – 2)

Exercise 1
1. widening   2. sharp decline / fall   3. general improvement   4. expansion   5. strengthening   6. tightening up   7. constant rise
8. dramatic increase   9. steady decrease   10. phased out   11. build up   12. cuts

Exercise 2
1. deterioration   2. considerable growth   3. upward trend   4. marked progress   5. broaden (*to broaden your horizons* is an idiomatic expression which means to increase your ideas, knowledge and experience)   6. upgrade   7. streamline   8. downsizing   9. slipped
10. fluctuated   11. amended   12. restructure

Changes 2 (page 3)

The words in the box are:
adapt replace expand increase promote reduce transform switch renovate exchange demote alter disappear vary raise lower extend enlarge heighten lengthen widen deepen shorten stretch revise fall outsource dissolve

1. exchanged   2. adapt   3. outsourced *or* switched (if a company or organization *outsources*, it uses workers from outside the company, or buys supplies from another company instead of producing them themselves)   4. transformed   5. renovated   6. switched   7. vary
8. expanded   9. dissolve (we could also use the phrasal verb *break up*)   10. revised (*revised* prices are usually increased, but they can also go down, as in this example)   11. promoted   12. extend

Comparing and contrasting (page 4)

1. contrast   2. differ   3. differentiate   4. characteristics   5. distinction   6. Compared   7. comparison   8. resemble   9. similarities
10. In the same way   11. Likewise   12. By way of contrast   13. Nevertheless / Even so / However (*Even so* is more common in spoken than in written English)   14. discrepancy   15. whereas

Computers and information technology (pages 5 – 6)

Exercise 1
1. desktop PC (PC = personal computer)   2. laptop (often called a *notebook*. Very small laptops are often called *netbooks*)   3. components
4. CPU   5. hard drive   6. hard disk   7. memory   8. software   9. word processing   10. spreadsheet   11. DTP   12. load (we can also say *install*)   13. CD drive   14. USB port   15. memory stick (we can also say *flash drive*)   16. monitor   17. keyboard   18. printer
19. scanner   20. mouse

Exercise 2
1. Internet (sometimes also called *the World Wide Web*, or just *the Web*)   2. provider (also called an *Internet Service provider*, or ISP)
3. access   4. browser   5. download (if you transfer information from your computer to, for example, a Web site, you *upload* the information)   6. chat rooms   7. Web site   8. log on   9. pop-up   10. search engine   11. keywords   12. links   13. homepage   14. on line (we often talk about *on line shopping*)   15. log out   16. bookmark (it)   17. email (sometimes written *e-mail*, *Email* or *E-mail*. The *e* is short for *electronic*)   18. spam   19. delete   20. attachment   21. virus   22. crashing   23. antivirus software   24. update

Condition and requirement (page 7)

1. As long as   2. Unless   3. on condition that (*that* = optional)   4. providing that (*that* = optional. We can also say *provided that*)
5. precondition   6. In case of (note that in this particular expression, we do not say *In case of a fire*. In other situations, an article or pronoun would be needed after *in case of*)   7. in the event of   8. stipulation   9. unconditional   10. Assuming that (*that* = optional)
11. on the assumption that (*that* = optional)   12. prerequisites   13. terms / conditions   14. requirement   15. Failing that (*that is* needed here, as it refers back to the previous sentence. *Failing that* means that if the first option – *telephoning us* – is not possible, you should try the second option – *send us an email*)   16. otherwise

Providing (that), provided (that), and *on condition (that)* are more formal ways of saying *if*.

Confusing words (pages 8 – 9)

Exercise 1
1. d   2. a   3. b   4. c   5. a   6. a   7. d   8. b   9. a   10. a   11. b   12. d   13. c   14. d   15. d

Exercise 2
1. b   2. c   3. a   4. b   5. b   6. a   7. d   8. c   9. a   10. a   11. c   12. a   13. d   14. b   15. c

Answers

Continuing, repeating and starting again (pages 10 – 11)

Exercise 1

1. ✓ 2. resume (*restart* could also be used here) 3. ✓ 4. revert 5. maintain 6. continual (<u>not</u> *continuous*, as the computer sometimes works and sometimes doesn't. *Repeated* and *constant* could also be used here) 7. continuous (<u>not</u> *continual*, as the tone makes one long noise without stopping) 8. ✓ 9. ✓ 10. persevere (*press on* could also be used here) 11. perpetuate 12. ✓ 13. reopen 14. keep up (*carry on* could also be used here) 15. persist 16. ongoing 17. ✓ (*continuous* could also be used here. A noise can also be described as *persistent* if it is repeated all the time: "*the persistent ringing of a telephone*") 18. ✓ (*progress* could also be used here) 19. steady 20. ✓

Exercise 2

1. repeatedly 2. continually 3. persists / carries on / continues 4. resume / restart 5. persevere 6. maintain 7. progressing / continuing 8. constant / continual / persistent 9. revert 10. Keep…up

Contracts (pages 12 – 13)

1.   1. parts = parties 2. False 3. C
2.   1. terminator = termination 2. True 3. obligated / required
3.   1. un-negotiable = non-negotiable 2. True (*amend = change* or *alter*. The noun is *an amendment*. You can <u>make an amendment</u>) 3. oral / spoken / implied / understood (Note that if a contract is *on paper*, it is called a *written* contract)
4.   1. in beach of = in breach of (*breach* can also be a verb: *to breach a contract*) 2. abide by (in paragraph 1) 3. False (Swilpot has only broken one of the *clauses*, or *parts*, of the contract)
5.   1. period of notification = period of notice 2. agreement 3. True
6.   1. anointment = appointment 2. False (*amalgamation* comes from the verb *to amalgamate*: to join and become one. We can also say *merger*, from the verb *to merge*) 3. False (he is not allowed to have a *controlling interest* in the company, so his ability to buy stocks is restricted) 4. None (*third parties* are people or groups other than Mr Wiley and the amalgamation of AKL Publishing and Berryhill Books)

Different situations (pages 14 – 15)

1. The speaker is explaining how to write a business / transactional letter. 2. They are at a conference. 3. Ms Akkabar is a dentist. 4. Staff training and development in his / her company 5. He's talking to someone (probably a receptionist or switchboard operator) on the telephone: he wants her to connect him to another person in the building. 6. The speaker is talking about his company's *staff appraisal* program. 7. The speaker has a (very) bad boss! 8. Ms Collins is explaining Mr Sheppard's *duties* and *responsibilities* at work. 9. Mr Sagala is a doctor (when we ask somebody how they *make their living*, we want to know what their job is). 10. They are looking at a bill or invoice for something.

Earnings, rewards and benefits (pages 16 – 17)

Exercise 1

1. salary 2. remuneration 3. overtime 4. increment 5. deduction 6. minimum wage 7. double time 8. pension plan 9. raise 10. advance 11. payslip 12. bonus 13. payroll 14. package 15. weighting (for example, a job advertisement might offer an annual salary of $40,000 + $5,000 New York *weighting*) 16. leave (or *vacation*) entitlement

Exercise 2

1. income / expenditure 2. satisfaction (often called *job satisfaction*) 3. commission 4. stock options 5. incentive plans 6. rate 7. redundancy pay 8. discount 9. relocation allowance 10. profit sharing 11. gross 12. net 13. index-linked 14. performance related 15. commensurate (for example, *Your salary will be commensurate with your experience and qualifications*) 16. golden handshake (some companies also give new employees a *golden hello* when they accept a job with the company)

Entertainment, art, sport and the media (pages 18 – 19)

(A) (The speaker is talking about a **newspaper** or a **current affairs magazine**) 1. circulation / readership 2. readership / circulation 3. coverage 4. events 5. features / articles 6. articles / features 7. researched 8. current 9. objective 10. lively 11. editor 12. journalists 13. Press

(B) (The speaker is talking about a **television news broadcast**) 1. technical 2. studio 3. anchor / reporter 4. reporter / anchor (in this context, an *anchor* is someone who presents the news on a radio or television programme) 5. off-screen 6. on air 7. live 8. network 9. complaints 10. broadcasting 11. break

(C) (The speaker is talking about a **novel**) 1. works 2. writer (*novelist* has a similar meaning) 3. Literature (*Literature* begins with a capital *L* here because it is the name of a particular prize) 4. plot 5. character 6. set 7. action 8. biographical 9. recommend 10. issued 11. anthology 12. copy

(D) (The speaker is talking about a **movie**) 1. director 2. box-office 3. Award (an *Academy Award* is also known as an *Oscar*) 4. actors 5. performances 6. effects 7. scenery / cinematography 8. cinematography / scenery 9. soundtrack 10. critics 11. release (we can also say *nationwide release*)

(E) (The speaker is talking about a **play**) 1. opening (we can also say *first night*) 2. audience 3. curtain 4. lights 5. stage 6. half 7. performance (a "part" of a play is called an *act*, so would also call the second half of a play the *second act*) 8. auditorium 9. cast (= *actors* in a film or play) 10. rehearsed 11. lines 12. dialog 13. scenery 14. backers 15. scriptwriter

Answers

(F) (The speaker is talking about a **museum**) 1. galleries   2. exhibits   3. ancient   4. acquired   5. collector (or collection)   6. art   7. collection   8. portraits   9. accomplished   10. artists   11. exhibitions   12. Admission   13. contribution (we could also say *donation*)
(G) (The speaker is talking about an **album** of **rock music**) 1. recordings   2. groups   3. note   4. track   5. fans / crowd   6. band   7. repertoire   8. hits   9. variations   10. studio   11. astute   12. crowd / fans   13. singer   14. compilation
(H) (The speaker is talking about a **sporting event** – in particular a **ball game** such as **soccer**) 1. supporters / spectators   2. stadium   3. teams   4. pitch   5. win   6. triumph / win   7. beat   8. opponents   9. captains   10. referee   11. cheerleaders   12. spectators / supporters   13. coaches   14. encouragement   15. score   16. draw

Food and eating out (pages 20 – 21)

1. (a) Customers / Diners (give yourself ½ point if you answered *Guests*)   (b) asked   (c) not   (d) restaurant   (e) want / would like   (f) go
2. Food should not be *high* in cholesterol (1 point) It should be *low* in cholesterol (1 point). The best way of preparing meat and vegetables is not by *frying* them (1 point): steaming and boiling (1 point for either of these words) are considered to be much healthier.
3. (a) goodness (or *vitamins* and *minerals*)   (b) ingredients   (c) rich in / high in   (d) minimum   (e) retain (we could also say *preserve*)   (f) wholesome   (g) preparing (although you do not always need to *cook* food to *prepare* it)   (h) free from   (i) artificial   (j) way
4. (a) to   (b) on / of   (c) down on / out (If you *cut down on* something you eat less of it. If you *cut out* something (from your diet) you stop eating it completely) / up (*cut out* and *give up* have the same meaning in this context)
5. ranger = range / organism = organic / additions = additives / modification = modified / fat = fast (*fast food* is also sometimes called *junk food* because it is not very good for you)
6. (a) recommend   (b) reservation   (c) service   (d) waiting   (e) portions   (f) diet   (g) undercooked   (h) rare   (i) well-done   (j) burnt*   (k) check   (l) overcharged   (m) service charge   (n) tip (we can also use the more formal word *gratuity*)

*Meat such as steak and lamb is usually cooked *rare, medium-rare, medium, medium to well-done* or *well-done.*

Hotels (pages 22 – 23)

Exercise 1
1. rates   2. single   3. twin   4. double   5. occupancy   6. supplement   7. family   8. suite   9. en suite   10. rates   11. quote   12. facilities   13. safety deposit   14. pay-to-view   15. Internet   16. amenities (we could also use *facilities* here)   17. residents   18. non-residents   19. room service   20. pool   21. business and conference   22. options   23. self-catering   24. bed and breakfast (B+B)   25. half-board   26. full-board   27. all-inclusive

Exercise 2
1. peak period (we can also say *peak season*)   2. advance   3. reservations   4. vacancies   5. email (sometimes written *e-mail*)   6. check-in   7. check-out   8. vacated   9. guests   10. charged   11. shuttle   12. transfer   13. guests   14. chain   15. Web site   16. staff   17. experience   18. training   19. competitive   20. uniform   21. chambermaids   22. housekeeping   23. receptionists   24. waiters / waitresses   25. waitresses / waiters (note that we often say *waiting staff* for men and women)   26. chefs   27. cashiers

Job advertising (pages 24 – 25)

Exercise 1
1. qualified   2. commission   3. motivate   4. incentive   5. responsibilities   6. cover letter   7. advance   8. rewards package (e.g., your salary, free health care, a company car, etc)   9. colleagues   10. post   11. résumé (this is a French word, so it is considered more correct to put the accent on both e's)   12. experience   13. vacancy   14. benefits   15. basic salary   16. team   17. interview   18. relocation allowance   19. application   20. commencing   21. leading (e.g., *a leading manufacturer of camera lenses*)   22. increment   23. drive   24. candidate (we can also say *applicant*)

Exercise 2
1. leading   2. vacancy   3. post (we can also say *position* or *job*)   4. commencing   5. application (the verb is *to apply*)   6. candidate (we can also say *applicant*)   7. qualified   8. experience   9. team   10. drive   11. motivate (the noun is *motivation*, the adjective is *motivated*)   12. colleagues (we sometimes use the informal word *workmates*)   13. responsibilities (we can also say *duties*)   14. rewards package (we can also say *benefits package*)   15. basic salary (note that a *salary* is the money, or *pay*, you receive every <u>month</u> or <u>year</u> for doing your job; a *wage* is money you receive every <u>day</u> or <u>week</u> for doing a job   16. commission   17. incentive   18. increment   19. relocation allowance   20. benefits (we can also say *rewards*)   21. advance   22. résumé (sometimes called a *curriculum vitae*, or *CV*, in British English. A résumé lists your qualifications and experience in detail, and also provides important personal information – name, age, contact details, etc)   23. covering letter   24. interview (A person <u>attending</u> an interview is called an *interviewee*; a person <u>conducting</u> an interview is called an *interviewer*)

Answers

Exercise 1

Part 1

1. vacancy   2. hire or recruit   3. staff   4. advertises   5. post or position   6. internally   7. externally   8. agency   9. work (job is countable, and should be preceded by an article or pronoun)   10. description   11. applicant   12. applying   13. requirements 14. qualifications   15. experience   16. qualities (we can also say *attributes*)   17. practical   18. professional   19. rewards or remuneration   20. salary (a *wage* is paid daily or weekly)   21. raises / increments (with a slight difference in meaning: a pay *raise* might be the result of promotion or hard work, an *increment* is usually automatic and based on length of time with the company.)   22. benefits 23. leave or vacations (*leave* is more formal)   24. package (we often use the expression a *rewards and benefits package*)   25. commensurate

Part 2

1. résumé (CV = *curriculum vitae*, and is usually only used in British English   2. cover (in American English) covering (in British English) 3. fill in or fill out (we can also say *complete*)   4. application   5. submit or send (*submit* is more formal)   6. short list   7. attend   8. reject or turn down   9. unsuitable   10. candidates or applicants   11. potential   12. appearance   13. disposition   14. skills or abilities 15. interests or hobbies   16. background (we can also say *circumstances*)   17. medical   18. suits or matches (although *matches* is the best word)   19. profile or criteria   20. offered   21. references (the *referees* in this situation are the people who write the references) 22. employer (although if you have come from a managerial position in another company, one of your employees might be asked to say what you are like as a manager)   23. colleague or co-worker (we can also use the less-formal *workmate*)   24. induction   25. temporary 26. trial or probationary   27. permanent   28. appraisal

Exercise 2

1. (a) qualifications   (b) job   (c) advertised   (d) experience   (e) internally
2. (a) description   (b) advertisement   (c) remuneration / salary   (d) apply   (e) qualities   (f) applicant / candidate
3. (a) raise   (b) professional   (c) unsuitable   (d) probationary / trial   (e) vacancies / jobs / work   (f) résumé   (g) reference

Location and direction (pages 28 – 29)

Language of location and direction is particularly useful if you take the *TOEIC Test of Spoken English*, where you may be required to describe where places are on a map, and explain how to get to them.

A. City Hall   B. Easy Street   C. fast food restaurant   D. nightclub   **E. The movie theater**   F. Park lane   G. Central Avenue H. Telegraph Road   I. deli   J. tourist information office   K. railway station   L. bus station   M. Stallone Street   N. library   O. Commercial Street   P. department store   Q. post office   R. museum   S. Luigi's restaurant   T. art gallery   U. Grand Hotel   V. Clemenceau Avenue W. Washington Park   X. Dominion Street   Y. shopping mall   Z. Marlene's bar

Linking ideas (page 30)

1. B, C, D (*Therefore* cannot be used because the second sentence is not a result of the first)   2. A, C, D   3. A, B, D (*Along with* needs to be followed by a noun or an –ing verb)   4. A, D (*Likewise* cannot be used because the second sentence is a result of the first sentence. *Because of* needs to be followed by a noun or adjective + noun: "*Because of a drop in sales, we had to close the department down*") 5. A (*In brief* is used to summarize what the speaker thinks, and usually follows a list of facts)   6. C (*Together* would also be correct if it was followed by *with*: "*...together with half the sales staff*")   7. A, B (the second sentence is a result of the first sentence)   8. A, B, C, D (these expressions are usually followed by a noun or an adjective + noun)   9. D (an informal expression, which you would normally only use in spoken English)   10. A, B (*also* is usually used before a verb and is not usually used at the end of a sentence)   11. A, C (*However* and *Nevertheless* are not usually used before a verb)   12. A, D (The second sentence recommends action as a result of the first sentence)

Meetings and presentations (page 31)

1. open   2. welcoming   3. participants   4. attendance   5. supporting   6. agenda   7. progress   8. schedule   9. get through 10. achieve   11. goals   12. objectives   13. chair (we can also say *preside over*)   14. contribute   15. clarification   16. interrupt 17. issues   18. address (= *discuss / talk about*)   19. bringing up   20. matters   21. priority   22. summarizing   23. points 24. recommendations   25. open floor   26. opinions   27. closes   28. notes   29. minutes   30. report   31. complaints   32. questions 33. floor

Money Matters 1 (page 32)

Exercise 1

1. If you **lend** money, you let someone use your money for a certain period of time. If you **borrow** money, you take someone's money for a short time (usually paying *interest* – see number 19) and then *repay* it. (Note that you *lend* money <u>to</u> someone, and you *borrow* money <u>from</u> someone).
2. **Inflation** is a state of economy where prices and wages increase (= *go up*). **Deflation** is a reduction of economic activity.
3. A **discount** is the percentage by which a full price is reduced in a shop (if the reduction is very big, we can say that it is a *bargain*). A **refund** is money paid when, for example, returning something to a shop (you will normally need to show a *receipt* when getting a refund – see number 8). Note that *refund* can also be a verb: *to refund money*.
4. **Income** is the money you receive (your *wage* or *salary* is part of your income). **Expenditure** is money you spend. Most people would like their income to be greater than their expenditure.

Answers

5. If a company is **insolvent**, it has lost all its money. If a company is **bankrupt**, it has lost all its money, it has also borrowed a lot, and it cannot pay back its *debts* (= money it owes). Being bankrupt is a very serious financial situation for a company to be in. (Note that a company *goes* bankrupt, or is *declared* bankrupt in a court of law. *Bankrupt* can also be a verb: "*the current economic situation has bankrupted us*")

6. A bank **statement** is a detailed written document from a bank showing how much money has gone into and come out of a bank account. A **balance** is the amount of money you have in your bank account.

7. If your bank account is **in the red**, your *expenditure* has been greater than your *income* (see number 4), and so you have less than $0 in your bank account. If your account is **in the black**, you have more than $0 in your bank account.

8. An **invoice** is a note, or *bill*, sent to you to ask for payment for goods or services (it can also be a verb: *to invoice* someone for something). A **receipt** is a note (from a shop, for example) which shows how much you have paid for something.

9. When you make a **profit**, you gain money from selling something which is more than the money you paid for it. When you make a **loss**, you have spent money which you have not gotten back.

10. **Gross** profit is the profit you make *before* money is taken away to cover costs of production, labor, tax, etc. **Net** profit is the money you are left with *after* costs, taxes, etc, have been taken away (money which is taken away is called a *deduction*).

11. If you have been **undercharged**, you have paid less than you should have for goods or services. If you have been **overcharged**, you have paid too much.

12. Something which is **overpriced** is too expensive. Something which is **exorbitant** costs much more than its true value (we can also use the more informal word *extortionate*).

13. If you **save** money, you keep it so that you can use it later. If you **invest** money, you put it into property, stocks, etc, so that it will increase in value (the noun is *investment*).

14. A **wage** and a **salary** are both money you receive for doing a job, but a wage is usually paid *daily* or *weekly* and a salary is usually paid *monthly*.

15. **Extravagant** describes someone who spends a lot of money. **Economical** (= *frugal*) describes someone who is careful with money.

16. A **loan** is money that you borrow to buy something. A **mortgage** is a special kind of loan used to buy a house or other building over a period of time.

17. A **loan** is money you borrow from a bank, and a formal arrangement has been made with the bank for this. An **overdraft** is the amount of money you withdraw from your bank, which is more than there is your account. It is sometimes done *without* making an arrangement with the bank (although many banks offer their customers automatic *overdraft facilities*).

18. A **share** is one of the many equal parts into which a company's *capital* (= money that is invested in the company) is divided. People who buy them are called *shareholders*. A **stock** is an investment in a company represented by shares. (Note that in the United Kingdom, stocks are shares which are issued by the government).

19. **Commission** is the percentage of sales value given to a sales person in a company. **Interest** is the percentage that is paid to someone for lending money.

20. A **worthless** (= *valueless*) object is something which has no value. A **priceless** object is an extremely valuable object.

21. When you **credit** an account, you put money into it. When you **debit** an account, you take money out of it.

22. A **pension** is the money that someone continues to receive after they have retired from a job. **Redundancy pay** is the money that is given to someone to compensate them for losing their job when a company makes them *redundant* (= no longer needed). (Note that if you lose your job and cannot find another one, you can receive *welfare* (= money from the government)).

23. A **dividend** is part of a company's profits shared out among shareholders (see number 18). A **royalty** is money paid to the author of a book, an actor, a rock star, etc, as a percentage of sales (it is usually plural: "*Royalties are paid twice each year*").

24. **Tax** is money taken by the government from incomes, sales, etc, to pay for government services. **Duty** is a special tax that has to be paid for bringing goods into a country (it is often called *import duty*).

25. If you **deposit** money in an account, you put money into the account. If you **withdraw** money, you take it out of your account.

26. A **bill** is a piece of paper showing the amount of money that you have to pay for goods or services (for example, an electricity bill). A **check** is a bill that you receive in a restaurant.

Exercise 2
1. refund / receipt   2. overcharged / check / tax / exorbitant   3. statement *or* balance / overdraft / in the red / expenditure   4. gross / salary / commission / net / income *or* salary   5. bankrupt / redundancy pay / pension / invested / stocks *or* shares / worthless

Money matters 2 (pages 33 – 34)

1⇨ budget   1⇩ bargains   2⇨ profitable   3⇨ capital   4⇩ compensation   5⇨ down payment   6⇨ earnings   7⇩ sponsored   8⇩ cost   9⇨ assets   10⇨ owes   11⇨ rebate   12⇩ check   13⇩ subsidized   14⇨ finances   14⇩ fortune   15⇩ afford   16⇨ credit   17⇩ audit   18⇩ funding   19⇨ welfare   20⇨ yield   21⇨ deducted   21⇩ debts   22⇩ rate   23⇨ charge   24⇨ currency

Obligation and option (page 35)

1. required (not *mandatory* or *compulsory*, as these cannot be followed with *by*)   2. compulsory (*mandatory* could also be used if the helmet and equipment must be worn because of a law)   3. must (not *have*, as this must be followed with *to*)   4. have / need   5. liable (not *obliged* or *compelled*, as these must be followed with *to*)   6. forced (this is better than *obliged* or *compelled*, as it is stronger and suggests that the company has no other choice. Also, *obliged* and *compelled* are usually used when somebody makes somebody else do something)   7. exempt   8. Mandatory (this is better than *Compulsory*, as it suggests the checks must be carried out because of a law: see 2 above)   9. voluntary (not *optional*, as the gap is preceded by *a*, not *an*)   10. optional (not *voluntary*, as the gap is preceded by *an*)   11. alternative (used as part of an expression: "*We have no alternative but to…*")   12. obliged / required   13. obligation (note the adjective form of obliged / obligation = *obligatory*)   14. compelled (in other words, he felt that people were putting pressure on him to make him leave. We could also use *obliged*)   15. entail (we can also say *involve*)   16. need (used here as a noun. *Obligation* could also be used, but is slightly more formal)   17. essential (*vital* or *imperative* could also be used)   18. allowed (we can also say *permitted*, which is slightly more formal)

71

Answers

Opposites 1: verbs and adjectives (page 36)

1. succeed 2. hollow 3. permanent 4. sharp 5. punish 6. public 7. smooth 8. approximate 9. borrow 10. guilty 11. advanced 12. minor 13. shallow 14. amateur 15. present 16. artificial 17. accept 18. destroy 19. deny

The words in the shaded vertical strip are *compulsory* (= *obligatory*) and *voluntary*.

Opposites 2: adjective prefixes (page 37)

Exercise 1
unacceptable inaccurate inadequate disadvantaged disagreeable unattractive unauthorized unavoidable unbelievable uncertain uncomfortable incompetent incomplete unconscious discontented unconvincing incorrect incurable uneven unfair unfashionable dishonest disinclined illegal unlimited illiterate illogical unmarried immature immoral immortal disobedient disorganized impatient imperfect impersonal impossible improper impure unqualified (*disqualified* is a verb which means to make someone not able to do something: "*He was disqualified from driving for a year*") irrational irregular irrelevant irreplaceable irresistible irresolute irresponsible unsatisfactory dissatisfied insufficient unwelcome

Note that adjectives which end with –*ful* are usually made into their opposite form by changing –*ful* to –*less* (*thoughtful* = *thoughtless*, *useful* = *useless*, etc). *Helpful* is one exception to this rule (the opposite is *unhelpful*. *Helpless* has a different meaning, and means *not able to do anything*).

Exercise 2
1. D (= disinclined) 2. B (= dishonest) 3. C (= insufficient) 4. A (= irresponsible) 5. C (= unconvincing) 6. A (= inadequate)

Opposites 3: verb prefixes (pages 38 – 39)

1. unfolded 2. misquoted 3. dislike 4. misbehave 5. disobeyed 6. misplaced 7. miscalculated 8. unloaded 9. disconnecting 10. misjudged 11. misunderstands 12. disapproves 13. disallowed 14. misuses 15. discontinuing 16. displeased 17. mistrust 18. uncovered 19. unlock 20. misdiagnosing 21. misrepresent 22. disqualified 23. disproved 24. disagrees

Ownership, giving, lending and borrowing (page 40)

1. Property 2. landlords 3. allocated 4. provided 5. mortgage 6. donation (the verb is *to donate*) 7. possessions 8. tenants 9. loan (this can also be a verb: *to loan*) 10. contribute 11. leased (the noun is *lease*: *to sign a lease*)

The word in the shaded vertical strip is *proprietors* (= owners of a business)

Phrasal verbs 1 (page 41)

1. go up 2. end up 3. cut off 4. fill out (*fill in* has the same meaning) 5. run out of 6. called…off 7. do away with 8. subjected to 9. get through to 10. come up against 11. pulling through 12. went through with 13. looking forward to 14. falling behind with

Phrasal verbs 2 (page 42)

1. on 2. out 3. up 4. off 5. over 6. down 7. in 8. up 9. into 10. up with

Phrasal verbs 3 (page 43)

1. going up = going through 2. checking into = checking in (you *check into* a hotel, but you *check in* for a flight) 3. come up to = come up with 4. build about = build up 5. fall up = fall through 6. bring apart = bring together 7. dropping in of = dropping out of 8. falls for = falls to 9. coming through with = coming down with 10. came in = came into 11. takes to = takes after 12. turn round = turn up

Prepositions 1 (page 44)

1. on* (note that the date in sentence 1 is spoken "*the second of April*" or "*April the second*") 2. by (= no later than) 3. since 4. under 5. across (*around* or *through* could also be used in this sentence) 6. with 7. to 8. for 9. out (*away* could also be used in this sentence) 10. from 11. on 12. to 13. from 14. in 15. by 16. by 17. for 18. through (*for* and *throughout* could also be used in this sentence) 19. in 20. in

* When we talk about times and dates: *on* is used for days and specific dates (*on Monday / on 15 September / on Monday 15 September*); *in* is used for months, years, seasons and periods of the day (*in September / in 2005 / in summer / in the evening*); *at* is used for specific times (*at 7.30 pm*).

Answers

Prepositions 2 (page 45)

The correct preposition is shown in parentheses.
1. B (on)   2. A (between)   3. B (for)   4. C (under)   5. D (on)   6. C (until or before)   7. D (through)   8. C (on)   9. A (by)   10. D (from)   11. B (for)   12. C (of)   13. D (with)   14. C (in)

Sales and marketing (pages 46 – 47)

Exercise 1

1. cowded = crowded   2. nich = niche   3. brocure = brochure   4. opmarket = upmarket   5. reserch = research   6. advertiseing = advertising   7. campain = campaign   8. premote = promote   9. comercials = commercials   10. advertisements = advertisements   11. billyboards = billboards   12. plop-ups = pop-ups   13. mailshoots = mailshots   14. sponsership = sponsorship   15. endoarse = endorse   16. pont = point   17. retale = retail   18. pich = pitch   19. disconts = discounts   20. giveways = giveaways   21. dommestic = domestic   22. expot = export   23. raps = reps (a short form of sales representatives)   24. franshise = franchise   25. merchantising = mechandising   26. brant = brand   27. pakaging = packaging   28. cattalog = catalog (or catalogue)   29. hipe = hype   30. fat = fad   31. competiton = competition   32. canvince = convince   33. perswading = persuading

Exercise 2

1. catalogue (or brochure)   2. endorse   3. packaging   4. point of sale   5. pitch   6. fad   7. hype   8. competition   9. brand (often called branded goods)   10. discount   11. sponsorship   12. mailshot

Shopping and consumerism (pages 48 – 49)

1. (A) concessions (we can also say franchises)   (B) chain   2. (A) customers   (B) consumer   3. (A) charging   (B) cost   4. (A) spend (you spend money on something)   (B) paid (you pay money for something)   5. (A) credit   (B) debited   6. (A) discount   (B) offer (we can also say bargain)   7. (A) change   (B) exchange   8. (A) prices   (B) costs (also often called overheads)   9. (A) wholesale (we can also say in bulk. You make a bulk purchase of something)   (B) retail   10. (A) for sale   (B) on sale   11. (A) receipt   (B) bills   12. (A) check   (B) bill (note the difference in meaning of bill in 11 and 12)   13. (A) check (note the difference in meaning of check in 12 and 13. Also note that you usually only ask for a check in a restaurant or bar)   (B) charge (a charge card is also called a credit card)   14. (A) economical   (B) economic   15. (A) stock   (B) supplies   16. (A) served   (B) serviced   17. (A) demand   (B) supply   18. (A) merchandise   (B) purchases   19. (A) refund   (B) return   20. (A) staff   (B) team   21. (A) do (note that people go shopping or they do their shopping)   (B) made

Similar meanings 1: nouns (pages 50 – 52)

Exercise 1

1. agenda / schedule   2. accommodations / housing (note that in American English, accommodation can also be plural: accommodations)   3. discipline / order   4. assistance / help   5. drop / decline (fall could also be used)   6. faults / defects   7. opposition / resistance   8. proof / evidence   9. discount / reduction   10. proximity / closeness   11. appointment / meeting   12. customers / clients   13. work / employment   14. benefits / advantages   15. requirements / prerequisites

Exercise 2

1. acclaim / praise   2. code / rules   3. liability / responsibility   4. choices / options   5. overview / (short) description   6. staff / personnel (employees could also be used)   7. cooperation / collaboration   8. Customers / Patrons   9. terms / conditions (often used as one expression: the terms and conditions of the contract)   10. questions / queries   11. outlet (often called a retail outlet) / store   12. problems / complications   13. strategy / plan   14. priority / precedence   15. revisions / changes

Exercise 3

1. reviews / write-ups   2. advertising / publicity   3. charisma / (personal) appeal   4. categories / classifications   5. ending / termination   6. entitlement / right   7. caliber / intellect and ability   8. specialist / expert   9. assignment / job   10. notion / idea   11. proficiency / skill   12. achievement / accomplishment   13. ultimatum / final demand   14. disparity / difference   15. proceeds / earnings

Similar meanings 2: verbs (pages 53 – 54)

Across
1. audit   2. explain   5. reclaim   6. promote   9. assist   11. exhaust   15. assert   17. avert   18. dictate   19. obtain   21. influence   22. administer   24. generate   25. select   27. realize   29. relate   31. measure   34. ban   35. brief   36. verify   38. increase   40. consult   41. endorse   42. require   43. convey   44. deduct

Down
1. address   2. employ   3. award   4. disturb   7. ascertain   8. gather   10. substitute   12. accelerate   13. handle   14. regulate   16. attend   20. compensate   23. reserve   26. retain   28. imply   29. reveal   30. clarify   32. analyze   33. resolve   37. finalize   39. consent

Note that using a word with a similar meaning to another word does not always mean using that word in exactly the same way structurally or lexically. For example: you can "prevent a strike from taking place" or you can "avert a strike" (not "avert a strike from taking place"); you can "suggest something without saying it directly" or you can "imply something" (not "imply something without saying it directly"). In these examples, the words at the end are not necessary because their meaning is carried in the main verb. This is

Answers

one reason why you should always record words in context, and with an example that shows how they are used, so that when you use them yourself, you use them correctly.

Also note that some of these verbs can be used in more than one way. For example, you can _convey_ a message to someone, or you can _convey_ goods from one place to another.

Similar meanings 3: adjectives (page 55)

Exercise 1
1. mandatory   2. integral   3. efficient   4. compatible   5. obligatory   6. lengthy   7. inventive   8. important   9. disparate
10. prosperous   11. legitimate   12. voluntary   13. steady   14. exceptional   15. diverse   16. flexible   17. profitable   18. disciplinary
19. tedious   20. punctual   21. nominal   22. perceptive   23. modern   24. industrious

Exercise 2
1. vibrant   2. simple   3. resolute   4. luxurious   5. prospective   6. restricted   7. thriving   8. enduring   9. extensive   10. rudimentary
11. relevant   12. adequate   13. abrupt   14. outdated   15. overall   16. risky   17. abundant   18. narrow   19. inconsistent
20. inflexible   21. crucial   22. thorough   23. discourteous   24. scrupulous

Starting and stopping (pages 56 – 57)

Exercise 1
The words and phrasal verbs in the box are:
abolish   arise   back out   cancel   cease   closure   delete   deter   discontinue   dismiss   dissuade   embark   eradicate   establish
fire   freeze   inception   initiate   kick off   launch   outbreak   phase in   phase out   pull out   quash   quit   resign   retire   set off
set up   suppress   suspend   take off   take up   terminate   turn down

Exercise 2
1. terminated _or_ canceled   2. deleted   3. backed out _or_ pulled out   4. outbreak   5. set up _or_ established _or_ launched   6. embarking
_or_ setting off   7. suppress _or_ quash   8. eradicated   9. deter   10. dissuade / initiated   11. launched / take off   12. suspended   13.
took up   14. phased in / phased out   15. inception or launch / closure   16. ceased   17. retiring   18. quit (= informal) _or_ resign / fired
(= informal) _or_ dismissed   19. turn…down   20. freeze   21. discontinued   22. abolish   23. kick off (= informal)   24. arisen

Travel 1 (pages 58 – 59)

Exercise 1
1. abroad   2. vacation (note that in British English, people say _holiday_. A holiday in American English is a day when people do not have
to go to work: for example, Thanksgiving, Labor Day, etc)   3. mass   4. package   5. transfers   6. accommodation   7. travel agency (we
can also say _travel agent's_. A _travel operator_, or _tour operator_, is a company that arranges tours and usually sells them through a travel
agency)   8. brochure   9. destination   10. itinerary   11. both words can be used, but _book_ is more common   12. both expressions are
correct   13. both words are correct   14. both words are correct (_depart_ is more formal)   15. independent   16. flexibility   17. departure
18. airfare   19. E-ticket   20. both words are correct   21. confirmation (from the verb _to confirm_)   22. trip (an excursion is usually as
day trip somewhere as part of a vacation)   23. check in (_check-in_ is a noun or adjective: _He arrived at the check-in five minutes too late /
Go to the check-in desk two hours before your flight_)   24. terminal (a _terminus_ is a place where a train or bus ends its journey)   25.
Ticketless   26. valid   27. both are correct (_expires_ is more formal)   28. visa (note that there are different types of visa, including _entry
visas_, _transit visas_, _work visas_, etc)   29. embassy   30. traveler's checks   31. currency   32. exchange   33. deal (_bargain_ sounds strange
when preceded by _favorable_)   34. commission   35. insurance   36. vaccinations (The verb is _to vaccinate_. We can also say _inoculations_
or _immunizations_)   37. arrangements

Exercise 2
1. independent   2. E-ticket   3. airfare   4. Abroad   5. mass   6. Commission   7. exchange   8. vaccination   9. terminal   10. package
11. check in   12. Valid   13. booking / reservation   14. trip   15. confirmation

Travel 2 (page 60)

1. delayed   2. overbooked   3. tourist / coach (_economy_ is used in British English. _Club class_ is the same as _business class_)   4. embarkation
/ boarding (although _embarkation_ is usually used for ships, and _boarding_ is usually used for aircraft)   5. transit   6. domestic (we can also
say _internal_ for flights that go between airports in the same country)   7. round-trip (= _return_ in British English. A _one-way ticket_ is called
a _single_ in British English)   8. credit limit   9. crew (although _team_ might also be used as a more informal alternative)   10. commuters
(note that a _mile_ is a measurement of distance equivalent to 1.61 kilometers)   11. carrier / airline   12. comprehensive   13. All of these
are correct (although _eco-tourism_ and _environmental tourism_ often involve the tourist in actually doing something to help the environment
while he / she is in the host country)   14. SUV (= _sport utility vehicle_, often called an _off-roader_, or a _4X4 (four by four)_ in British English)

Word forms 1: nouns from verbs (pages 61 – 62)

Exercise 1

Remove 2 letters, then add 4 letters:	provide = provision persuade = persuasion recognize = recognition abolish = abolition decide = decision
Remove 1 letter, then add 7 letters:	qualify = qualification apply = application identify = identification notify = notification imply = implication
Remove 1 letter, then add 5 letters:	consume = consumption admire = admiration permit = permission determine = determination compete = competition
Remove 1 letter, then add 4 letters:	argue = argument assure = assurance intervene = intervention expand = expansion produce = production
Remove 1 letter, then add 3 letters:	negotiate = negotiation expose = exposure supervise = supervision (*supervisor*, a person who supervises, could also go in the section below) behave = behavior promote = promotion
Remove 1 letter, then add 2 letters:	refuse = refusal survive = survival (or survivor, somebody who survives) arrive = arrival rehearse = rehearsal respond = response
Add 3 letters:	fail = failure coincide = coincidence warn = warning suggest = suggestion prohibit = prohibition
Add 4 letters:	disturb = disturbance attend = attendance require = requirement manage = management (a manager is somebody who manages, eg, a company or department) prefer = preference
Add 5 letters:	sign = signature expect = expectation recommend = recommendation consult = consultation relax = relaxation

The 10 words that do not fit into any section of the table are:
choose, solve, emphasize, subscribe, scrutinize, justify, criticize, acquire, lose, maintain

Exercise 2
1. choice (from *choose*)   2. solution (from *solve*)   3. emphasis (from *emphasize*)   4. subscription (from *subscribe*)   5. scrutiny (from *scrutinize*)   6. justification (from *justify*)   7. criticism (from *criticize*)   8. acquisition (from *acquire*)   9. loss (from *lose*)   10. maintenance (from *maintain*)

The verb / noun in the shaded strip is *compromise*.

Word forms 2: nouns from adjectives (pages 63 – 64)

Exercise 1
1. value   2. ✓   3. thirst   4. honesty   5. ✓   6. expense   7. ✓   8. similarities   9. certainty   10. ✓ (or *absence*)   11. convenience   12. necessity   13. ✓   14. flexibility   15. ✓   16. responsibility   17. ✓   18. ✓   19. complications   20. difference

Exercise 2
Remove 4 letters: comfortable = comfort   fashionable = fashion   systematic = system
Remove 3 letters, then add 5 letters: long = length   high = height   strong = strength
Remove 3 letters, then add 1 letter: optimistic = optimism   pessimistic = pessimism   realistic = realism (*reality* is also a noun form)
Remove 2 letters, then add 5 letters: able = ability   available = availability   compatible = compatibility
Remove 2 letters, then add 3 letters: hot = heat   deep = depth   confused = confusion
Remove 2 letters, then add 2 letters: aggressive = aggression   creative = creation   appreciative = appreciation
Remove 2 letters: functional = function   logical = logic   optional = option
Remove 1 letter, then add 3 letters: considerate = consideration   mature = maturity   secure = security
Remove 1 letter, then add 2 letters: convenient = convenience   sufficient = sufficiency   true = truth
Add 2 letters: bored = boredom   loyal = loyalty   warm = warmth
Add 3 letters: familiar = familiarity   popular = popularity   punctual = punctuality
Add 4 letters: aware = awareness   serious = seriousness   weak = weakness

Answers

Word forms 3: adjectives from verbs (page 65)

1. promotional / inspiring   2. innovative / impressive   3. wasteful / obligatory   4. repetitive / boring   5. excited / doubtful   6. decisive / active   7. inventive / changeable   8. continual (= stopping and starting) / continuous (= without stopping)   9. approachable / frightening   10. convincing / critical   11. inclusive / competitive   12. helpful / supportive / dependable   13. rectifiable / preferable   14. negotiable / refundable   15. restricted / valid   16. voluntary / constructive   17. avoidable / careless (not *careful*)   18. creative / imaginative / admirable   19. specific / occupational   20. attractive / excellent

Workplace problems (page 66)

Paragraph (A)
1. dispute   2. resolved   3. strike   4. arbitrate

Paragraph (B)
1. timekeeping   2. absenteeism   3. misconduct

Paragraph (C)
1. fraud   2. discrimination   3. bullying   4. racial   5. abuse   6. sexual   7. harassment   8. fired   9. suspended   10. unfair   11. dismissal (we can also say *wrongful dismissal*)   12. appeal

Paragraph (D)
1. breaches   2. neglecting (this can also be a noun: *neglect* of duties)   3. insubordination   4. damage   5. disciplinary   6. board   7. instant   8. dismissal

Paragraph (E)
1. shortages   2. overstretched   3. grievance (= a formal word for *complaint*)   4. walkout   5. verbal   6. warning (after a *verbal warning*, an employee might receive a *written warning*)   7. notice (when a company *asks you for your notice*, they are politely telling you that they are going to force you to resign)

Paragraph (F)
1. dropped   2. redundant   3. resigned   4. bankrupt   5. hacked   6. virus   7. crashed   8. order (*out of order = broken / not working*)